The
PATH

A Market Maker's Financial Path to Spiritual Awakening

Matthew Roland Adams

BALBOA.
PRESS

A DIVISION OF HAY HOUSE

Balboa Press books may be ordered through booksellers or by contacting:

Balboa Press
A Division of Hay House
1663 Liberty Drive
Bloomington, IN 47403
www.balboapress.com.au
1 (877) 407-4847

Because of the dynamic nature of the Internet, any web addresses or links contained in this book may have changed since publication and may no longer be valid. The views expressed in this work are solely those of the author and do not necessarily reflect the views of the publisher, and the publisher hereby disclaims any responsibility for them.

Trading and or investing in the equity options markets have inherent risks. Anyone investing in options should be given a copy of the pamphlet "Standardized Risks in Options Trading" by their broker before opening an option trading account. The author and publisher will not be held liable for any losses incurred using the strategies set out in this work.

Any people depicted in stock imagery provided by Thinkstock are models, and such images are being used for illustrative purposes only.
Certain stock imagery © Thinkstock.

Print information available on the last page.

ISBN: 978-1-4525-2616-4 (sc)
ISBN: 978-1-4525-2617-1 (e)

Balboa Press rev. date: 04/28/2015

Dedication

To the Supreme God
To my Spiritual Guides
And to all those who trade the options markets worldwide
May this book bring you onto the Path of
Financial and Spiritual Awakening

Acknowledgments

To my wife Rosann and daughter Adriana
for your love and support
To my father Emmett and mother Winifred
for wisdom beyond imagination
To Ellen, Allison and Martin - siblings don't
have to get along. You're wonderful beings.
To the American, Pacific and CBOE exchanges for
lessons that allowed me scope to pursue my path
To all the great teachers and spiritual beings that are helping
and blessing us constantly out of love and compassion

Contents

Preface

In 1984 when I became a member of the American Stock Exchange, there were six Black American members out of about 1200 members in total. Yours truly was the only Black market maker trading on the floor at that time. The others worked for brokerage firms. The experience of being in that type of environment was bittersweet. To actually be able to use things like statistics in a dynamic working environment instead of through book study gave me a new understanding of mathematics and its uses in the so-called real world.

This diary is a beginning. The term "distilled knowledge" is another way of describing experience. To watch the Dow Jones industrial average climb from 770 in 1982 to 2700 in 1987 was amazing. To actually be trading on the floor when the '87 crash occurred is the kind of experience that you tell your great-grandchildren. Everyone knows the market went down 508 points that day, but if you were on the floor the following morning you got to see something most of the public missed. The futures indicated that the market would open down another 700 points. That would have been, shall we say, interesting.

The stock exchange floor was home for a lot of us for many years. It wasn't just the trading; it was the fellowship. Being a member of an exchange was something to be proud of.

It's truly sad that greed and desire will ultimately take the floor away. Regulators want to regulate and in this day and age computers allow those authorities to account for every transaction seamlessly. Gone are the days when you and the specialist could stand around and trade for half a point because everyone kept the markets in line. We now live in the days where every single action has someone looking to make money. The spreads between bids and offers get tighter and it's called progress. You're told it's better for the customers. New rules are implemented for the efficiency of order execution. Once again you're told it's better for the trading public.

It's better actually for the regulators who are made up of lawyers and accountants who want to litigate and make someone accountable. Learning about trading and/or investing is something that can bring freedom to the masses. The question is what will then happen to the accountants who have nothing to account for, the lawyer with nothing to litigate and the regulator with no one to regulate.

We all must play the game for a while. The problem is most people don't know the rules for winning the game. And once you've won, what do you do next?

This diary is an opportunity to take a look at equity options trading from the floor perspective. All order flow goes to the floor. Those who work there learn to look at markets with a view towards providing fairness, speed and efficiency.

There was no time to use fancy computer software to price options. We used a better tool, the most efficient tool a human being has, the brain.

Knowing the foundational strategies gives you unlimited power and potential. Don't be fooled by the simplicity. As Master Choa Kok Sui, the modern day founder of Pranic healing and Arhatic Yoga, would say,

"The deeper the teaching, the higher the truth being told, the simpler it seems on the surface."

Matthew Adams
2015

Introduction

March 1982 Harlem: Doral Bar 145th and 7th Ave.

There is something about walking through Harlem that just relaxes me. Knowing how this neighborhood used to be and its future potential is just soothing. Remembering how I'd hang out at Grandma and Grandpa's place on 153rd and Amsterdam at holiday time and then head down the hill to the so-called seedier side of Harlem, away from the safe confines of Sugar Hill. Wondrous!

The Doral Bar on 145th Street and 7th Avenue was a meeting place. It was a place where I could talk to my Dad, relax and enjoy. Ultimately it was a philosopher's corner. You'd discuss the day's happenings and of course wait to see what was leadin'… the numbers were and are a part of Harlem. We may not know what is happening with the crazies in D.C. politics but we all know what's leadin'.

I'd sit and talk with my Dad and his friends. Ballantine Ale was the drink of choice.

"Hey D.O.D. (Dear Ole Dad), just got a job on the stock exchange." "Yeah? Ha! That's a good one, Matt."

"What-da-ya mean?" His friend Bev chimed in, "That's the snake pit." I asked Bev his meaning. He gave me the first lesson of many that my Dad and his buddies would impart.

"A snake pit has many different kinds of snakes. Some are poisonous and some aren't, but if you stay in there long enough, you'll get bitten by both."

Then D.O.D. said, "Now you'll get to see how they treat each other. Matt, remember one thing, you'll see soon enough that as long as you're no threat, you'll be OK. As soon as they see you can play their game, number 1: they try to get rid of you and number 2: they change the rules.

"Remember what that old man said to you down at St. Patrick's Cathedral when you told him about going there for an interview? He was surprised? Why? Because young Black men aren't supposed to do that. Just remember what can happen. Do the best you can and don't call too much attention to yourself."

That last piece of advice would cause a lot of conflict for me down the track but... the intention was loving and honorable. After that it was time for another ale. Besides, Maynard had just entered the bar, so now the conversation would shift to city politics and the troubles of retired police officers.

1

A view from the balcony

March 1982 – American Stock Exchange, New York City

The Interview: I was going for a job as a reporter on the exchange floor. Met with exchange management reps Joe Tandy and Richard Monderine. Our meeting was pretty straightforward. The job paid $276 a week plus benefits. There would be a raise to $300 per week in about three months. I took the job offer and had to start training the following week. Richard took me down to the floor for the first time. We followed many pathways from the upper offices and reached the balcony where the clerks worked. That balcony was two stories up with small staggered booths going up another two stories to the ceiling.

I looked out over the expanse of that trading floor. The energy of the place was quite foreign to me. The noise level and the men and women in different colored jackets walking about were an alien energy indeed. Richard said, "You can go as far as you want to go, Matthew. You can become a member of this exchange if you want to. It's up to you."

I found myself remembering a story my father told me: "Matt, when I was about four years' old my mother's helper, Mother Philip, had a vision." Mother Philip was clairvoyant. "She told my mother that she saw the Devil on the stock exchange floor cracking a whip over the market participants. That should tell you where you're going to work. By the way, Matt, that was about 1928 or '29 and you know what happened then."

So now a person, who used to pass the financial section of the *New York Daily News* faster than a Ron Guidry slider, was working on the floor of the AMEX.

Financial Markets, especially equity option trading, have been described in many ways. The most common is a boring mathematical mine field for those whose life revolves around probabilities, not possibilities. The experience of trading on the floor of a stock exchange, with all of its characters, is something that I will forever cherish. The reason for that is, for me at least, profound.

2

Money dynamics

Doral Bar

My father and his friends used to throw questions out around the bar to see who was in tune with the happenings of the day. From sports to politics, from jazz to women, everyone had an opinion.

I threw out the question: "What is money? Or should I say what is money, really?" I got many answers.

At one level, money is the medium used for exchange of goods and services. Money is more than that, however. At this point in time, we must all recognize what money truly is. Throughout history we have been told the stories of the barons of industry and how they built empires of massive wealth.

From childhood we've heard stories of Howard Hughes, J. Paul Getty, Aristotle Onassis, and of course the Rockefellers, Kennedys, Vanderbilts, Rothschilds and so on. They are rich beyond measure, controlling vast amounts of wealth worldwide. They know what money truly is. Yet what most people don't realize is that for people like that to control the wealth they control, they need others, willingly or not, to accept less than they are truly worth.

Why?

"Money is Energy: Every day we wake and go to work, we exchange energy for money."

We are all energy beings that take birth in a physical body, live and die. No exceptions. We all have a finite number of breaths that we are allowed to take while here on earth. We all breathe the same thing, oxygen. Our energy is life force.

Therefore what makes one person's physical body worth more or less than another's? What makes one person's thoughts and feeling more or less valid than another's? What do we all expend daily? Energy… What makes one person's life energy worth more or less than another's? On the mundane level, the job they do during their working hours.

So we put a value on a person's life force. We now can tell a person what their life is truly worth in monetary terms based upon what they're paid for an average eight-hour work day five days a week. It's fascinating to think that part of society has become so petty that it will value a person based purely upon the work they do supporting the infrastructure that has been set up by a government and the current power brokers.

What's even more fascinating is that people allow this to happen. Why? Most people deal with a lack of valid source information. We in the so-called Western world are all born in the same condition more or less. Over the years, we are fed information that will ultimately shape the way we react to stimuli around us.

Governments and the rules of law not only control the way we live but also try to control how we react to stimuli. This government and those rules are entities that we've created. They now have an energetic life of their own.

They don't want to die prematurely. In order for government to survive, the infrastructure must thrive. In order for the infrastructure to thrive, there must be people to maintain it. In order for the people to maintain it and all of its support mechanisms, those people must be willing to sacrifice part of the value of their life force to government control. We've created a huge genie and now we are responsible for feeding it.

Infrastructure: I find this word and topic quite interesting. Government infrastructure must be maintained. What is it anyway? A Google search provides the following definition: The basic facilities and services for the functioning of a community or society, such as transportation and communications systems, water and power systems and public institutions. It is also the basic framework or features of a system or organization.

Some might say that the people have made a choice to support something supposedly greater than self. Was that choice made with valid source information? Or, given all the facts, would they have made a different choice with their life force?

Doral Bar: Jimmy Devil walks in with what's leading. F-O-U-R, four is leadin' people. There's a low rumble as half the place tears up their tickets.

This afternoon's topic is education. My father asks me a question. "Hey Matt, what was the best course you did at Pace University?" "Honestly, it was a history course on the Indigenous Peoples of America and how every single treaty that the U.S. Government made with them was broken. The textbook's title was *The Long Death*. I still have it if you want to read it." "Nah, I pretty much know about that one. What does that tell you?" "It told me that we're not the only people to get screwed in this country." Bev starts laughing. "Why did you like the class so much?" "Because it was an account of what happened from the so-called American Indian perspective. Natives would even come to class and speak about their experiences. It was real. Not a story told by the perpetrator." "So it was a true education?" "Yeah, from the source."

That class was the best class I took at University. I still remember reading and hearing about how the government manipulated every situation, taking more and more from the natives back then. This was the truth and at many levels I truly appreciated the fact that the truth was still being talked about aloud.

3

Real education

Why is education, true education, so important? True education allows us to properly validate information given to us by different sources. True education teaches us that life force is abundant on the earth. If that is the case, and money/energy is what drives world economies, why isn't money or energy management being taught to children at the beginning of their development?

Because true knowledge allows us to go beyond the limits of this existence and create massive amounts of wealth or energy, which does not necessarily serve the purpose of governmental infrastructure. Take a look at a wealthy person and you'll be looking at someone with control over a massive amount of life force.

What does money afford us? In a word, time. Enough money gives us back those eight-plus hours a day to do other things. More importantly it gives us something else: choice.

Choice beyond the normal constraints this life will throw at us. We all work a certain amount of time and get between three and six weeks vacation every year. That means on average we spend 72 (24-hour days) out of 365 days per year at work or about 20% of our adult life per year.

That 20% finances the other 80% of life. So the salary you receive from your employer gives you an approximation of what your employer thinks your life energy is worth to them. If the average income in the US were $31,500 dollars per year, it would mean that the average American's life force is valued at about $3.60 per hour.

The life force of the typical person in India with an average salary of $US500.00 per year would be about six cents per hour. Japan would average about $5.13 per hour. Australia would be about $2.72 per hour in US dollar terms. Most people would think that their time is worth more than that. Compare that with a person earning $US500,000 per year and you get about $57.23 per hour. A lot better…

It's interesting to note that the continent with the most natural resources on this planet, Africa, values life force the least in dollar terms or should I say the Western world values that life force the least. One African country has a value of 1.7 cents per hour.

As we begin to recognize monetary/energetic value, we begin to understand how the world of investing truly works. What are we actually investing in? We are investing energy into something that will be able to add more life force to our money, making it multiply.

By placing money into stocks, bonds, commodities, and cash deposits, we are taking our energy and putting it into a place where we hope it will be energized and allow us to benefit. The key after that is what to do with the extra energy.

Right now the US and Europe's monetary energy is lethargic. The Australian was trading near ten-year highs so its monetary energy is high. Investors worldwide are moving their lethargic energy into an energy stream that is vibrant and invigorated. The monetary energy of the US and Europe needs to regenerate itself. How? How do our bodies regenerate? We have to recognize that everything we create will go through a period of growth and rest – in financial terms, economic cycles.

So we are attempting to put our energy in the form of money into an enlivened stream of energy that we hope will make our energy multiply.

When it comes to investing that means learning how to play the game.

Doral Bar: *"Hey Pee Wee what's leadin'? Six is up. I'm in there. You get your cut from Bobby last week? Yeah, it's about time he hit one. All right gentlemen I'll see you later. Work to do… See ya Bev."*

I asked my Dad what Bev meant about his cut. "Remember one thing, Matt, when you win, you give. We all share it around when we win. You win 6 and you give out 2. That's how it goes." The noise level in the bar starts to build. Jimmy Devil and Big Deal walk in. "Hey Deal, what's second? Three people. 6-3." My dad smiles and buys another ale. He's still in it and he just won $360.

Jimmy Devil asks me how it's going on the floor. I tell him it's going well. It's a learning process. He asks me, "Tactics, Matt, what are your tactics?" My father is looking at me and waiting for my answer as well. I had to think about it. What was my plan for a typical trading day? "In a place like that you gotta have a plan. Hope you're using that meditation you do."

I used to separate spirituality and business. It seemed that spiritual matters weren't meant for use on the floor of an exchange.

As I said this, my Father started laughing. "Man, you gotta be kiddin'. Did you read that copy of the Bhagavad Gita I gave you? Krishna had it all, including wealth. Everything comes from God, Matt, including money. I ask God for more money every day. Just because you meditate and follow a spiritual path, doesn't mean you have to be poor. That money you make pays for your meditation classes, right?"

From that point on I brought my meditation practices out of hiding and allowed that energy to help me on the floor as well.

4

Tactics

Trading Tactics

1. Physical surroundings
2. Access to market information
3. Trading Platform
4. Physical Energy
5. Mental Clarity

Physical surroundings

As you trade, how are your physical surroundings? Are you in a space that allows you to concentrate on the job at hand? Make sure that your trading surrounds support what you are doing. The beauty of the stock exchange floor was that all necessary support mechanisms were at your fingertips.

Access to market information

You'll need up-to-the-minute information on leading economic indicators and company announcements. Services that give you twenty-minute delayed news and quotes are of no use to traders. Trading past news is a waste of time.

Trading Platform

There are many trading services that now offer trading systems that allow the average investor access to all they would need to trade properly: Live quotes, sub-second trading, news and charts. Most systems out there allow for sophisticated order entry as well: Contingency orders, stop/stop limit orders, trailing stops, Market-on-close etc…

The trading platform you choose must allow you to access market information and trade on that information quickly and efficiently. If you are trading the US market for the first time you will find that commission costs are kept to a minimum. Take a look at brokers' websites to see what charges are involved when trading.

Physical Energy

Never trade tired! Always make sure you have enough energy to trade the market in a state of alertness. Never trade and drink alcohol! Just as law enforcement tells us not to drink and drive because it affects your awareness and reaction time to things going on around you, the same rules apply when trading markets. Alcohol definitely slows down your reaction time to market events.

When you're done trading for the day or evening, you should be energized by your activity, not tired. That leads to the final point:

Mental Clarity

Before you start trading always check your mental state.

Your state of mind while trading will have a dramatic effect on all aspects of your trading.

Clarity of Mind will lead you to have the proper physical surroundings to trade in.

Clarity of Mind means you'll know how to interpret all market information at your disposal.

Clarity of Mind allows you to navigate your trading platform with ease and efficiency.

Clarity of Mind means you'll never forget to make sure you have enough energy to get the job done.

Clarity of Mind leads to clarity of purpose. Clarity of purpose leads to *not second guessing* your trading strategies because you've put in the work and understand the risks.

Clarity of Mind while trading equates to a higher trading efficiency and more money being made.

Mental Clarity is something we as investors must be vigilant about. It takes practice and thought and will lead to a larger equity balance.

5

Never mind why, just do it!

As time passed, I got used to the trading floor and its nuances. Before long it was commonplace to be in the mix with the market makers, $2 brokers, and specialists.

When I think back on that time, there was so much going on that I missed out on a lot of great wisdom. It's the way of things. Like when you're growing up and your father tells you that those shoes you want to buy so badly are just a fad and you should get something sensible. You don't care about what is sensible, you want the Playboys.

It's the same thing with trading the markets especially options. I was lucky. Once I started to trade, there were people around who truly helped me. My trading partner at the time told me what to do on that first day. *Buy 20 XMI March 235 calls and sell 12 futures against them.* I bought the calls and before I could sell the futures the Federal Reserve cut interest rates. The calls doubled in value. Welcome to the floor...

The Floor – As I walked along the balcony overlooking what seemed to be a mass of confusion, Richard turned to me and said, "You can take this as far as you want to. You can become a member of this exchange. It's up to you." Choice... It's all about the choices we make. As US citizens we can make that choice.

Our constitution supposedly says so. What happens after that choice is made is anyone's guess. We all have the capacity to learn the nuances of trading in the financial markets. What matters the most is our input source.

At its current level of development, Western civilization relies on source information from the Fourth Estate in its many guises: Satellite, Internet, Cable and Radio all provide the source information we need to evaluate market conditions on a global scale. All of this information used to have a central hub as far as finance was concerned.

6

The Exchange Floor

The New York Stock Exchange: Founded in 1792, it is the largest and most prestigious equity floor in the world. Located on the corner of Broad and Wall streets, it is still the financial center of our universe.

The American Stock Exchange: circa 1921 New York Curb Market: the other side of Broadway on Trinity Place. A Stock and Option Exchange that helps the NY financial district maintain its dominance.

The Chicago Board Option Exchange: Founded 1973, it is Equity Options' true home. The CBOE standardized the options market. Van Buren St. in Chicago strikes again. Along with its creator, the Chicago Board of Trade, it helped to cement Chicago as the second city.

Philadelphia Stock Exchange: Founded in 1790, the First Stock Exchange. Located on Market Street. The New York Stock exchange charter was based on this model. Close enough to New York City to still be considered part of the East Coast triumvirate.

Pacific Stock Exchange: Founded circa 1862, the first Stock exchange to build an electronic trading system. The first option exchange to demutualize.

Boston Stock Exchange: Founded 1834, it was the first US exchange to allow foreign broker-dealers and banks to have membership privileges.

From a US point of view, the stock exchanges have a rich and revolutionary history. If we were to look at the pricing of securities back in the 18th and 19th century, then we would find that today's price for a company like Berkshire Hathaway was commonplace. The stock exchange floor is a place for buyers and sellers to transact business under the eyes of a so-called third party or witness. Market places like these are part of the backbone of our country's economy.

These stock exchanges are competitive. They vie for business on many levels. A New York firm might want its order flow directed to a New York Market as opposed to one in Chicago. A client in Philadelphia might want to trade on the Philadelphia Stock Exchange instead of the CBOE even though both exchanges list the same product. So these exchanges are in competition with each other for our business. Because of this the US market has some of the best commission rates in the world. Back in 1982 1.5% commission on a stock trade was commonplace. Now discount brokers have commission rates no one could have thought possible, but what about the rest of our planet?

While the US is the be-all and end-all to the average American, it's not the case as far as the rest of the world is concerned. They believe their markets are just as viable while still acknowledging US financial dominance.

London Stock Exchange: Founded 1760, and regulated 1801. London and New York are recognized as the world's financial centers. When we talk of NY we mention the Dow Jones; when we talk of London we mention the FTSE index. The words are part of the world's vocabulary.

Tokyo Stock Exchange: Founded 1878. With a history of wartime strife, the 11 stock exchanges in Japan were unified in 1943 and dissolved in 1947. All security trading was suspended in 1945 due to war conditions. Trading unofficially restarted in December 1945 but the revised Securities and Exchange Act didn't come about until April 1948. Three exchanges were established in Tokyo, Osaka, and Nagoya. And now Japan has five exchanges.

Hong Kong SAR (China): Founded 1891. A combination of two exchanges, the association of stockbrokers in Hong Kong and the Hong Kong Stock Brokers Association, became the Hong Kong Stock exchange formally in 1947 re-establishing the market after WW2. Hong Kong, along with exchanges Shanghai and Shenzhen, form China's marketplace.

Australian Stock Exchange Ltd. A coming together of six stock exchanges: Melbourne founded in 1861, Sydney founded in 1872, Hobart founded in 1882, Brisbane founded in 1884, Adelaide founded in 1887 and Perth founded in 1889.

We are currently seeing a major shift in the way the world's stock exchanges work. The word demutualisation is sweeping the globe. Depending on your political philosophy, this can be boon or bane. Demutualisation and/or mergers decrease competition while creating a more efficient market place.

Physical trading floors are disappearing and computers are taking their place. This may be more economically efficient but what are we losing? As a member of an exchange who would physically trade on the floor, I can say that there are things that I would and do miss.

So why are things changing? To what end? The answer is the same as it was 150 years ago, Money, the way it's controlled, and who does the controlling. By now you will have noticed the pattern. It's called the no witnesses policy.

7

World view

Ganeshpuri India 1994

While living in Gurudev Siddha Peeth ashram in India, I was asked a question about my life back in the US. It was a question whose answer would reveal itself over the next ten years.

The question was "Why don't you trade for others?"

As a market maker on the floor of a stock exchange in the US, you have a Broker–dealer license. This license allows one to trade on the floor for one's own account. You are not allowed to act as agent for others. We are not financial advisors or stockbrokers, although some of us did have series 7 and series 63 licenses. We use our own money and add liquidity to the marketplace.

Ten years after being asked the aforementioned question, I've come to realize that I made the right decision to trade that way. It took me ten years, because to truly understand why I made that decision I had to try and trade for others. In a nutshell here's my view.

1. Only trade for others if they are qualified investors who are able to invest in a plan for 5-10 years at a minimum.

2. All others should be left alone to run through the maze of brokers, mutual funds, newsletters, accountants, financial planners, regulators, technical analysis, fundamental analysis, financial news networks, websites and the like.

Most people are not well-heeled enough to commit to a true investment plan. If they have one it's usually out of fear. The "I must do this or I'll have nothing for retirement" investment plan. Their minds fluctuate from stocks to real estate at the drop of a hat or a well-placed article in the newspaper extolling the virtues of one over the other.

Most people have been brainwashed to believe that their lives must run with linear precision marching them to retirement age. Question, what is retirement age? I am of the opinion that we should make as much money as possible now.

The reason the banks and brokerages treat their clients like they do is because they know how fickle their clients can be. The sweaty masses have just fallen to sleep and allow brokers to control it all. Then a story comes out in the media and panic or greed set in. Well, the brokers don't mind at all. And the salaries they make show that the people are clueless.

It's all marketing. And especially in America, if it's packaged right and has good spin they'll buy just about anything. On the other side if you talk about it like a rabid junk yard dog they'll abandon it so fast it'll make your head spin.

8

Government – there's the rub!

We in the Western world should stop and look at the way we live. It will answer a burning question that people have. Why is it so hard to break free? Answer – the governments of the Western world need their populations to support the infrastructures that are now in place. What would happen if we all made millions in the stock market at the same time on a ridiculous investment like, oh let's call it the... Internet?

Unless everyone agreed to continue working, the infrastructure would fall apart. Governments cannot allow the working middle class to break free, retire early and head for the beach. Who would maintain the roads, bridges, and waste water treatment facilities? Who would police, who would fight fires, who would sweep the streets, drive the buses and trains etc...? If the bus drivers of the world all made millions buying Internet companies, they could actually pay off their mortgages. What if all working class people could do the same thing?

But the banks and mortgage companies would just love it. Or would they? Who would they then loan money to? The next tier down perhaps. But that would be risky and the people who own stock in the banks wouldn't like that too much. That would drive prices lower on those companies. So the banks don't want you to break free either. Hmmm!

And if the governments truly wanted the best for its slaves … uh… citizens, then why aren't we able to put 60k or 100k or 500k per year into our 401k, Keogh and/or IRAs and Superannuation pre-tax?

If you made a million dollars and only needed $75,000 to live on you'd be able to defer 925K that year to your retirement. Why is it that the pre-tax maximum for a Keogh is about 40K? Because that means that the government would get to tax you on 885K at around 30%.

You could take the balance after tax and put that into an annuity.

That's if your accountant doesn't talk to you about estimates for the next year. You know, that's where you're asked to pay an equivalent amount of tax based upon the amount you just finished paying, on a quarterly basis. If you're in that situation, kiss another 67K goodbye every three months until the following year. Insurance companies cannot afford people to stop working early, which would lead to less stress and longer life. Pharmaceutical concerns would cower at the thought of people living longer and healthier lifestyles, taking away from the sale of antacids and other so-called medicines for stress relief. Oh yes, less stress would also mean less ulcers, heart disease, and cancer. If that were to happen in the US, the government would once again have to lift the age for collecting social security to about 75.

Just ask yourself these questions:

How much money would I save if I could work from home or retire early?

How much would I save on car wear and tear?

How much would I save on gasoline?

How much would I save on food?

How much would I save on clothing?
How much would I save on stress?
How much would I save on insurance and taxes?
Or you could say:
How much less would the car mechanic make?
How much less would the gas company make?
How much less would eateries make?
How much less for clothing stores?
How much less for insurance companies?
And how much less for federal and state governments in taxes?

9

Trading and/or Investing

Stocks

Most public investors deal with stocks, equities or shares. It is
the easiest introduction into the market place for most people.
The first thing to be aware of is that stock ownership comes
with responsibility. What are you buying and why are you
buying it?

*1st responsibility – "We are responsible for our choice to purchase
stock in a company regardless of how we've come to that decision. We
cannot blame anyone else for this choice but ourselves."*

Ever read the disclaimers at the bottom or back of just about
every newsletter, report, or analysis about stocks, bonds, and
mutual funds? What is being said? We have to take responsibility
for the choices we make. To that end, we come to the next
responsibility.

*2nd responsibility – "We have to form a solid investment
foundation by being familiar with the companies we invest in."*

I personally have heard more rumors about different stocks
from the public sector than I've ever heard on the floor of the
exchanges of which I was a member. Cab drivers in Australia give
you stock tips. Your neighbor has a friend whose father works

with the daughter of the director of XYZ Company and they just heard that…

It's amazing. Always start with something you're familiar with. What services do you use every day? Who makes your washer and dryer? What make of car do you drive? What phone company do you use? Who provides power to your home? Who receives payment when you drive on a toll road? What brands do you buy constantly?

If there is a service that you swear by, look into investing in that company. You already know their product, its reliability, and how the company's staff supports the product. That is where you begin.

3rd Responsibility – *"We are investing in these companies to make money by capital appreciation and dividends. The key words are to make money."*

We have to remember why we invest. It's not some divine vision of the future. It's not to support a company and the economy. It's not to support the government and its infrastructure. It's to make money to use as we see fit. If we're honest with ourselves, that is why we invest. One of my teachers told me something that rang true for me. It's one of those statements that you hear and once you've heard it, you know it is true:

"Money is the representational value of your personal energy by those in a position of authority."

If we spend a quarter of our life working or exchanging personal energy for money, is it any wonder why people feel the way they do about money and the stock market. The stock market is a place where the personal energy of millions of people comes together. Why? To hopefully increase the value of the personal energy those people have expended.

If people feel that their personal energy, in the form of money, has been undervalued, that feeling or thought form will attach itself to their money and consequently to their investment. Imagine all the thought forms attached to all those investments out there, all vying for the same thing, recognition in the form of increased energy value.

What must be realized is that we call it many names: saving, investing, planning for the future but in fact what we are doing is simply trying to build our energy stores. Survival. We want to live and in order to do that in Western society we must eat, rest, clothe and shelter ourselves. We therefore work and exchange our energy for money.

So stocks represent a way for people to hopefully increase the value of their energy by putting part of their, in most cases, undervalued energy into the place ruled by the authority holders. Remember another name for the stock market is the secondary market. That leads to a question 'down the road'. See Chapter 11.

Once we understand what money is and how it is valued by different entities, our attitude towards investing takes on new dimensions.

If I can invest in a company and make a 200% return on investment in a year, which is 196% more than a bank would pay on savings, would I take that profit? This question leads to the next responsibility.

4th Responsibility – "I must learn to take profits and losses without guilt, greed, praise or blame."

I heard a story about an investor in Australia who invested in a stock that was trading at a price of .27 cents. The investor purchased 100,000 shares of this company. The company rose to a price of $19.90 and the investor did nothing. This person did not want to sell the company because of the capital gains taxes. This person no longer has to worry about that because the stock is now in receivership.

You invest $27,000 Australian dollars and watch it grow to be almost $2 million in one-and-a-half years and allow the stock to go under? That is a person that places no value on their personal energy at all. They still own the company's stock. This investor still has a profit but at what cost? There are many stories like this one all over the planet. The lesson that comes from such stories is another truism by a teacher of mine. "In order to be successful, one must have constancy of aim and effort."

The key is to know what and where your target is. Most investors buy companies and hold them. Why? They were told that's the way to invest in stocks. We have to realize that Buy/Hold is just one of many stock strategies. If your personal needs are being met, if you have no mortgage or car notes and you have extra money (energy) to invest, that might be the strategy for you. If you are in need of extra income, have a mortgage and kids to care for, waiting years for stocks to appreciate will lead to a stressful situation especially in down markets.

10

Stock investing is really about...

Stock investing is really about putting your energy to work for you to make yourself happy. This leads to another truism about money. I first heard this from a good friend in India in 1994.

We were in Thana at a restaurant called Shiv Prasad having the businessman's lunch. Cost 110 Rupees.

It was an extremely hot time of the year, about 120 degrees Fahrenheit in the shade but we were in air-conditioned comfort. My friend Charles looked up from his meal, turned to look at the people outside in the heat and said, "Matthew, money is time." I looked at him with a please-go-on look.

"We're sitting here enjoying life because we have purchased the time to do so. Money, our expended energy, allows us time to be here enjoying a meal thousands of miles from home. It will allow us to fly to Cairo or Bangkok or up to Lhasa if we so desire. Our energy allows us this because we conserved and honored the energy we've been given."

Money gives us time to pursue that which makes us truly happy. If we deny ourselves that happiness, those in the position of authority, through their agent the stock market, will take that energy back. When we've learned to honor and control our energy in the form of money, we have control over time itself. Most people have a very hard time understanding this concept. When you invest and make money, you must buy yourself something. Whether you buy a new house, car, watch or just go on a vacation, reward yourself with something of substance. By doing this you'll be able to look at that item or time and know that you have traded successfully. Believe me there'll be enough time for trading commiserations. Honor yourself; you are worth it.

11

Down the road

Do you believe that "those in a position of authority" would relinquish that authority willingly?

The Tech Wreck in the late '90s was very interesting. The Internet came into its own. Young entrepreneurs were feasting on the fruits of their labors or lack thereof. I noticed that most of the so-called "old economy companies" were not really interested in this phenomenon. It was a fad that would fade with time.

To say that tech stocks debuted on the markets with meteoric rises is an understatement and a half. The prices were truly crazy in my opinion but all of that is not really important. What was important was that people were making money. You would think that's a good thing. Well, that would depend on which authority you talked to. I received phone calls from friends all over the US saying that their retirement accounts and personal investing accounts were doing so well that they would be able to "pay off their houses and retire." Receptionists who received stock options as a bonus found themselves with million dollar stock holdings. Police officers, bus drivers, trash collectors, and teachers literally had control of their own destiny. So what happened?

Those in authority through another one of their representatives, the main stream media in its many forms, went to work.

Well-placed words in financial newspapers, Market Gurus on financial television shows with an axe to grind or a newsletter to sell were spouting statements like: "These companies have no hard assets to speak of." "This is pie in the sky. There is no foundation for these investments."

When the backbone of infrastructure a.k.a. the general populace, are in a position to be liberated from authority *en masse*, something must be done to keep them in their place. The tech companies that were feasting saw famine in the form of 80–100 percent drops in value.

People were no longer talking about paying off the mortgage. They were now in a position of loss. But… that's not the point. The true point is that people were given an opportunity for financial freedom and in most cases they did not take it. Why? They did not practice constancy of aim and effort. Those prices were real. You could have bought Qualcomm at 200 and sold it at 750. Did you? The financial industry is in flux at present.

We are seeing people and regulatory agencies go after the mutual fund and banking industry over trading tactics. It makes the masses feel good

"Ah, you see, Martha, they were doing something wrong. I knew it." The fact is that most people cannot truly commit to trading, let alone investing properly. Why? Because the equity they are using for their future years is needed to fund their present lifestyles. For an investor who knows equity options or is willing to learn, volatile markets are a Godsend.

12

Option Trading

Calls Puts: Content vs. process

The Leverage Factor

Options trading can be one of the most lucrative areas of investing. Options are leverage pure and simple. I will talk about exchange-listed options here. Many working folks don't have the time to watch markets on a daily basis. Working takes precedence over investments. We have financial advisors or brokers to do the work for us in most cases.

Options are fast-moving instruments and for the investor who doesn't have the opportunity to track the market daily, the option strategies implemented should be limited because of market risk.

Options – With Options you can initiate a position by buying or selling. There is no need to own an option before you can sell it. You can "sell to open" an option position.

Buying options – You have rights with no obligations; i.e. Buy 5 XYZ December 10 Calls.

You have the right to purchase 500 (US) or 5000 (Australian) shares of the underlying security at a price of $10 (strike price). You don't have to buy the stock. You have a choice you can implement depending on market conditions in XYZ.

Selling options – You have an obligation to do something; i.e. Sell 5 XYZ December 10 Calls. Depending on market conditions you may be called upon to deliver XYZ stock at 10 (strike price).

So when we buy options we have rights and choices. When we sell options we have obligations that we agree to meet under certain market conditions.

13

Calls and Puts

Buy Call - the right but not the obligation to buy the underlying security.

Buy Put - the right but not the obligation to sell the underlying security.

Sell Call - the obligation to sell the underlying security at the strike price if the security is above the strike price at expiry.

Sell Put - the obligation to buy the underlying security at the strike price if the security is below the strike price at expiry.

As with a lot of things in life, we pay for our rights. In the world of options, the price we pay for the right to buy/sell the underlying security is called premium. If we take on an obligation or responsibility we receive payment for that in the options world. We would receive or be paid a premium.

That option premium is made up of two parts.

1. Intrinsic Value
2. Time Value

Intrinsic Value: The true value of any option based upon its price relationship to the underlying security. If stock in ABC is trading at $25.00 and the ABC December 22.50 calls have a price of $4.00, the intrinsic (true) value of the option is the difference between the strike price (22.50) and the stock price (25.00) or $2.50.

Time Value: In the above example there is still $1.50 left over. That $1.50 is time value. Time value is directly linked to the amount of time the option has until it expires. In the case of an option expiring in December 2014, at the time of this writing, we would have, let's say, six months worth of time value. The price of that amount of time is therefore $1.50.

So the basics for options are:

    a. You can initiate a position by buying or selling
    b. Buying gives you rights with no obligations
    c. Selling gives you an obligation under certain conditions in the underlying security
    d. You either pay or receive a premium depending on buying or selling
    e. That premium is made up of intrinsic (true) value and time value

14

Strategies

A lot of times when you pick up a book on trading the market, it's hard to make head or tail of the information being given. Most of us are trying to find some synonymous form that makes us feel that there's hope. Well, markets can be painfully blunt when it comes to the lessons it teaches. Option trading is something that has to be experienced. To just read about it won't give you that confidence you need to be successful.

The Indian Guru Baba Muktananda would say "When you have something to do tomorrow, do it today. When you have something to do today, do it now. When you have something to do now, do it."

True trading confidence comes from taking right action. Right action is not paper trading or watching another person trade. Right action is to have your own direct experience of the markets.

Options: Buying Calls/Puts

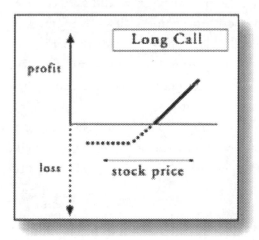

My first trade on the floor of the American stock exchange was buying calls. I had worked as a specialist clerk for one-and-a-half years and was now a member of the exchange. My partner told me that my first trade should be a Backspread. I was to buy 20 call options on the XMI index and sell the underlying future against those options. The sheer awesomeness of finally trading as a member of the exchange was enough to make me forget everything I knew about options and trading. My mind had gone blank. I couldn't remember what a call option was. In a sense, it was great that I was told what to do. I just did it and that was that.

As it happens, before I was able to sell the futures against my purchase, the Federal Reserve announced a cut in interest rates. The options I had purchased took off. I looked at my trading sheets and saw a $16,000.00 profit. With this came the realization that I really needed to learn about trading. It wasn't in a theoretical textbook that the answers would come.

Analysis: The market was trending upward. I purchased call options first. The second trade was to be selling the futures so

I traded with the trend and it paid off. It was through direct experience that the true answers would surface. It was fortunate that I made money trading in the first few months. It gave me the cushion I needed to learn how to trade properly.

Anyone who was around in '87 knows that owning puts can be lucrative. When the market is moving up, people are happy. Some folks take 10% profits; others wait for more. The key is that people are making money. When the market goes down… everyone wants out at the same time. It's times like that when owning puts can be the greatest thing since sliced bread.

Options: Selling Calls/Puts

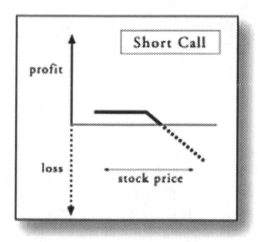

I'm not a call seller by nature. I've known quite a few traders who are, however. On the floor there were many times that market makers would just sell 100 calls at 1/16 ($US625.00) towards the end of the month to collect the premium. I can remember many floor traders who would sell options like this frequently. It worked for them most of the time however, during certain months it was an absolute bloodbath. The options they sold for $625.00 were worth $38,000.00 by the end of the trading day. That was rough. It was even harder watching them scramble to cover the positions.

A lot of people talk about the fact that options sellers make a lot of money. You must add the statement "10 months out of the year" to that. Those other two months are hellish for them. Take a look at a stock like CME. The Chicago Mercantile Exchange has done quite well in the past. The stock has made a run from the mid-sixties to over 600. It has since fallen back to the 130s after a trip down to 115. The stock then reached $250 dollars per share before falling below 80 again. What would happen to a person that looked at that company and decided to sell the three month

90 strike price calls when the stock was 80? The key here is risk. Selling calls naked has unlimited risk.

My trading mentor made a statement to me and I follow it to this day. "Matthew, never be net short puts." Don't get me wrong, selling puts can make people a lot of money but God help them when the market is going down. Short-term puts is where everyone goes to "protect" their positions and that means the put sellers get hammered.

What I've found over time is the following:

In volatile markets: Buy premium (Back Spreads)

In quiet markets: Sell premium (Front Spreads)

In low-key trending markets: Sell premium (Front Spreads)

In frenetic trending markets: Use caution

15

Analysis

"When a man does not know what harbor he is making for, no wind is the right wind." Seneca

Market analysis has confounded men for decades. Depending on the world economic climate, analysis will change. There are times when the bond and stock markets move in tandem. There are other times when the bond market and gold move as one. Then there's the time when a company announces earnings, they are stellar, and yet the stock goes down because analysts thought the earnings would be higher.

How many times have we heard the words of the news reporter at the end of the day's trading? "After a weeklong rally, the share market was down today on profit taking." Or "Market jitters after Federal Reserve chairman's address to Congress."

What is market analysis really about?

A so-called expert is supposed to be able to give you information about a certain company or a certain market sector and you're supposed to jump through hoops to get to buy these companies based on these recommendations. These experts spend many years studying and researching companies to allow us to make the best-informed investment decision. For what? A salary and prestige?

We are all supposed to read up on all of the stocks we invest in. We should all have foreknowledge or the best information at our disposal so that we will increase our return on equity. An analyst gives information for what? A fee. If an analyst of a brokerage firm can perform above and beyond the call of duty, their firm will get more business hence more commissions.

If that same analyst has a cold spell it could cost their firm business, which is why you'll find that most of the analysis done on stocks by different firms is pretty much the same.

One firm just can't afford to stand out and possibly be wrong.

Out-performance of the market is the key to attracting assets. Even if the market is down 20% and the firm is down only 15% on their recommendations, they've done their job. They've out-performed the market. With all of the troubles at brokerage firms lately, regulators now want to have separate analysis departments so there won't be a conflict of interest. Analyzing a company takes on new meaning these days. With all that happened in WorldCom and Enron, are the numbers being disseminated for real?

Technical analysis – Many of us just love our charts. Candlesticks, Kagi, line, bar, and many other charting patterns make your lives that much more exciting.

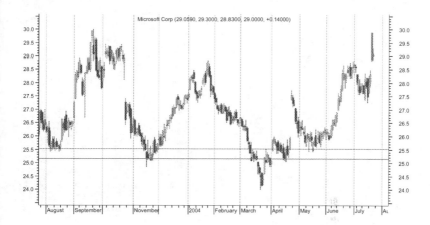

Fig.1 Candlestick Chart source: Metastock professional

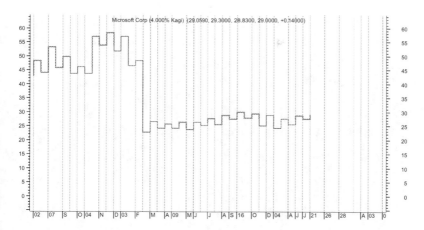

Fig.2 Kagi Chart source: Metastock professional

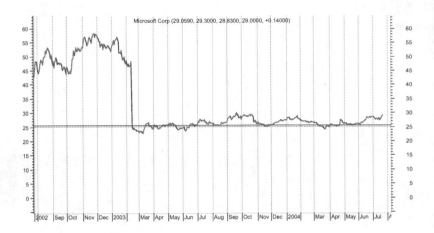

Fig.3 Line Chart source: Metastock professional

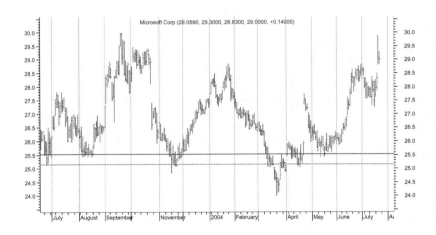

Fig.4 Bar Chart source: Metastock professional

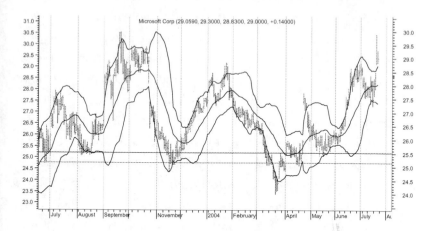

Fig.5 Bar Chart with Bollinger Bands

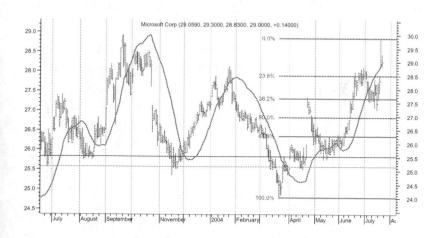

Fig.6 Bar Chart with Moving Average & Fibonacci
levels source: Metastock professional

We all just love drawing moving averages and Bollinger bands. We live to see what secrets Fibonacci will reveal this day. Will the Gann lines give a better evaluation or will I go with Elliott wave?

Charts do give us a picture of the market. Charts, to the chagrin of fundamental pundits, also give us all of the fundamental data needed to make a trading decision. When a company announces earnings, it shows up in the charts. When a company has a news announcement, it's in the charts. Everyone's hopes and aspirations are shown in the charts. Being that every possible piece of information is in a chart, why is it that people still struggle to interpret that information?

The answer is because all of the information is there including our hopes, dreams, fears, anger, lust, greed, and sentiment. Our ego tends to rule our trading habits. When you walk into an Indian temple there is usually a shoe rack just outside the entrance and next to it a sign that says before entering "leave your ego with your shoes." Egoless trading is something that has to be mastered to become successful in the market.

When we look at a chart we must become detached. We must learn to see what is going on and then make a decision based upon the information presented, not our opinion of that information.

16

Fundamental Analysis

Fundamental analysis tells us how a company is performing based upon accounting principles. We like having opinions on just about everything so when it comes to trading, we also have an opinion. Fundamental data provides a financial opinion on a company's financial health and well-being. If you don't think it's an opinion, look at Enron. Once again analysts will interpret this information based upon criteria set forth by the firm they are working for and by how a company's numbers compare to its peers in their industry.

When a company reports earnings or dividends it can have dramatic effects on share prices. We use different analytical tools to help us decipher "new information". The way money managers interpret new information is the main factor for stock market fluctuation. That new information can be company related, stock market related, bond market related, money market related, or world economy related.

Mutual fund managers, hedge fund managers, and economic forecasters have massive amounts of market power. We follow some of their recommendations religiously. Instead of millions of people with differing opinions buying and selling shares, we now have an elite few controlling money for the masses. We have given fund managers permission to act on our behalf. They've harnessed energy (money) on a grand scale.

Sound fundamental principles assume sound business principles. Fundamental analysis uses a form of propositional logic that allows us to form an opinion on a company. I say a form of propositional logic because it's not just the old if... then... system. It's the since... and... then... system. *Since* XYZ had earnings of .30 per share for the last six months *and* it should increase those earnings by 10% for the next six-month period *then* we believe the stock has a price target of...

Any time this kind of system is used you must recognize that new information changes all assumptions. My father used to say, "That's the beauty of economics, you're never wrong." Based on certain conditions, we should perform this way or that way. Change the conditions and we'll perform that way or this way. What mattered for market makers trading on the floor was when earnings would be announced, when the stock was going ex-dividend, any pertinent information that can have a dramatic effect on the company's stock price and how that information will be interpreted by the masses.

If you want to invest for the long term, fundamental analysis can help immensely. Any stock that you purchase in a retirement account should be evaluated using fundamental criteria.

Sound money management principles state that the financial health of a company is paramount for making long-term investment decisions. So what do you use? Which combination of fundamental numbers will unlock the secrets?

Price/Sales Ratio
Price/Earnings Ratio
Earnings
Book Value
Price/Book Ratio

Price/Sales: The market value♦ of the company divided by its sales

Price/Earnings: The market value♦ of the company divided by its earnings

Earnings: The sales of the company minus the company's expenses (Income Statement)

Book Value: The assets of the company minus the debt of the company. (Net Worth)

Price/Book: The market value♦ of the company divided by its book value

♦*The Market value of a company is the company's current stock price multiplied by the number of shares outstanding in the marketplace.*

Once you've worked with these numbers you still have to trade. That's where the overvalued or undervalued component kicks in. What are the historical norms that will allow you to gauge a company's performance?

Expensive: Two times book value and 20 times earnings.

Cheap: One times book value and 10 times earnings.

There are many other numbers that you can look at to determine a company's value. One tool I find invaluable is the COT (commitment of traders) data. This is data that shows whether the professional investors are buying or selling and which sectors of the market they currently favor.

Question: If I purchase the stock of a company in my retirement account with a goal of achieving a 200% return over the next 20 years and the company achieves this goal in two years, do I keep the company's stock or do I take the profit from that trade and invest it elsewhere? What would you do?

17

A view from the inside

Market Maker's view – A market maker knows one thing with certainty: new information will come into the market place consistently. This information will be interpreted in many ways depending upon personal agendas so they must react quickly, no matter which way, to market movement.

Since we cannot predict order flow, we must learn to be reactionary. To that end there are certain things that must be known to trade effectively.

THIS IS THE CORE OF WHAT OPTIONS ARE. THE GOAL IS TO MECHANICALLY WORK WITH THIS UNTIL IT BECOMES INTUITIVE...

THE SYNTHETICS, CONVERSIONS, REVERSALS, THE BOX.

You must have a solid foundation or the building will fall. The solid foundations for options trading are: the synthetics, conversions, reversals, and the box. If you know these, your foundation for options trading will be build out of granite.

Synthetic relationships: The synthetics are a must for successful option trading. The relationship a call or put has to the underlying security and to each other is paramount to trading success.

Synthetic Long Stock Position –
Buy (Long) Call + Sell (Short) Put

Matthew Adams
Foundational Option Strategies

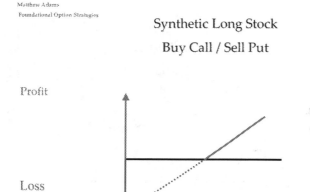

Synthetic Long Stock
Buy Call / Sell Put

The synthetic long can be a more efficient way to use capital than a direct purchase of the underlying shares especially for long term holdings in growth companies. LEAPS and LEPOS are long dated options that should be looked into for this purpose.

Copyright© 2002-2007
Higher Spheres Inc.

Allows participation in the underlying security with all the profits to the upside and losses to the downside. Participation will terminate on the date of expiry of the options. In the case of a stock that is priced at $40.00, one would pay $40,000.00 dollars for 1000 shares. By purchasing one call and selling one put with the same expiry date and strike price, one would be able to control 100/1000 shares (USA/Australia) of the underlying stock at a reduced rate.

Synthetic Short Stock Position –
Sell (Short) Call + Buy (Long) Put

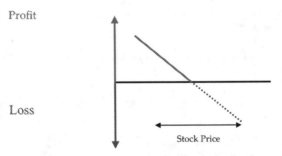

Matthew Adams
Foundational Option Strategies

Synthetic Short Stock

Sell Call / Buy Put

Profit

Loss

Stock Price

If your financial advisor has a problem with you shorting physical shares then remember the synthetic short position using options.

Allows participation in the underlying security with all the profits to the downside and losses to the upside. Participation will terminate on the date of expiry.

Synthetic Long Put
Sell (Short) Stock + Buy (Long) Call

Matthew Adams

Foundational Option Strategies

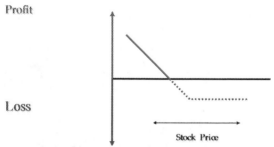

Synthetic Long Put

Buy Call / Short Stock

Profit

Loss

Stock Price

When done in ratio it becomes a backspread. Great risk management tool. When stocks move violently you'll love having these positions.

Synthetic Short Put
Buy (Long) Stock + Sell (Short) Call

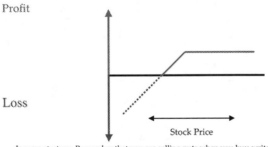

Matthew Adams
Foundational Option Strategies

Synthetic Short Put

Buy Write

Buy Stock / Sell Call

Profit

Loss

Stock Price

Income strategy. Remember that you are selling puts when you buy-write. That means unlimited downside risk.

Synthetic Long Call
Buy (Long) Stock + Buy (Long) Put

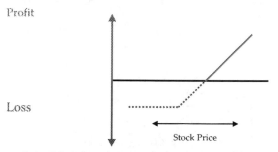

Matthew Adams
Foundational Option Strategies

Synthetic Long Call
Buy Stock/ Buy Put

Profit

Loss

Stock Price

Buying Calls gives us unlimited upside potential with limited downside risk. If you have long term stock holdings and are worried about the downside, synthetically create puts for protection.

Synthetic Short Call
Sell (Short) Stock + Short (Sell) Put

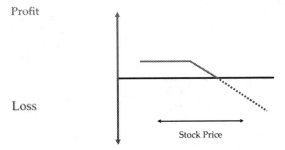

Matthew Adams
Foundational Option Strategies

Synthetic Short Call

Short Stock / Sell Put

Any naked short call position has unlimited risk. Be mindful of this when selling any premium.

I cannot over-emphasize the importance of knowing these relationships. They are the foundation for all option strategies that are implemented on option exchanges worldwide.

What if we could synthetically buy (sell) a stock for less (more) than the actual stock is trading for? We could then sell (buy) the underlying stock and lock in a profit. What if after looking at this we now knew that the synthetic stock has to be equal to the underlying issue or we could always profit from the disparity?

Reversal:

Buy ABC MAY 35 CALLS
Sell ABC MAY 35 PUT
Sell ABC stock Short
With the reversal we are synthetically buying the stock using options and selling the underlying issue.

Conversion:

Buy ABC MAY 35 PUT
Sell ABC MAY 35 CALLS
Buy ABC Stock

With the conversion we are synthetically selling the stock using options and buying the underlying issue.

When doing this we need to know if the stock will pay a dividend during the options life.

If a dividend is to be paid over the period we hold the position:

Conversion (Long Stock) will receive the dividend and Reversal (Short Stock) will pay the dividend.

We will also need to know the cost to carry the position. Options trade in a margin account so while we hold the position we will pay interest conversion (Long Stock) or receive interest reversal (Short Stock).

The Basic formula to calculate this is:

Strike price (35)* Days to expiry (trading days until the options expire)* interest rate/ 365(for the conversion) or 360(for the reversal).

Buying the Box

Buy Box

Strike Price		
25	**Buy Call**	**Sell Put**
30	**Sell Call**	**Buy Put**

Buy Synthetic Stock lower Strike/ Sell synthetic Stock higher strike.
Value = difference between strike prices ($5.00) Same expiry month.

You synthetically purchase and sell stock at two different strike prices in the same month of expiry. When buying the box you purchase the stock synthetically at the lower strike price and sell stock synthetically at the higher strike price.

ABC
BUY MAY 30 CALLS
SELL MAY 30 PUT
And
BUY MAY 35 PUT
SELL MAY 35 CALLS

This position is always worth the difference between the strike prices, in this case $5.00 if you can buy the box for less than the difference between the strikes you keep that difference.

Selling the Box

Sell Box

Strike Price		
25	**Sell Call**	**Buy Put**
30	**Buy Call**	**Sell Put**

Sell Synthetic Stock lower Strike/ Buy synthetic Stock higher strike. Value = difference between strike prices ($5.00) Same expiry month.

Copyright© Matthew R. Adams

When selling the box you sell the stock synthetically at the lower strike price and buy the stock synthetically at the higher strike price.

ABC
SELL MAY 30 CALLS
BUY MAY 30 PUT
And
BUY MAY 35 CALLS
SELL MAY 35 PUT

If you can sell a box for more than the difference between the strike prices, again $5.00, you keep that difference.

Once these are mastered you find that pricing options becomes a lot easier. You also begin to understand that in spite of all the hype about the newest computer generated "implied volatility" pricing models from the mathematical universe...

If a stock is currently priced at (x) Dollars, its synthetic long and short equivalent must be equal to (x)and the volatility numbers must reflect this as well.

Implied volatility, a futile attempt at present value, helps us to price the time component of options but it still cannot violate the relationship rules that options have to the underlying instrument they are based upon or the relationships that call and put options have to each other.

Knowing the synthetics and learning the uses of conversions, reversals and boxes, gives option traders one of the most solid foundations available. Working with these and learning to use them to interpret markets opens you up to possibilities you didn't think existed in options trading. They are the true cores of options understanding. Implied volatility tells you what price the market is willing to pay for time "in the present moment". That can change dramatically, based upon new information. The bias with options is selling premium. Look at it from the point of an insurance policy. We pay a premium to an insurance company to protect our lives, cars, houses, health, business etc. This company is just selling a call option on those things. It's that with the insurance policy, the strike price is death, a car accident, a house fire, flood or robbery, a broken leg or burst appendix, or a business mishap.

You'd then exercise your policy and the insurance company would have to deliver; usually, in the form of money.

Therefore most option investors sell premiums to collect money because they believe that, just like the insurance companies, they'll get to keep the premium most of the time. The trouble is that when violent things happen you get destroyed. Ask an insurance agent how they feel about hurricanes, floods and tornadoes.

18

It's all Greek to me

Option investors learn the world of the so-called Greeks to help them value options and establish positions.

Delta: (γ) Equivalent Share Position (E.S.P.)

Expressed as: Positive number for calls
Negative number for puts

An options delta tells the investor how many options it will take to equate to the underlying security. If we were to purchase an XYZ call and sell an XYZ put in the same month of expiry with the same strike price, we would have the equivalent position of buying the underlying security. The call and put would each have delta.

If our call option had a delta of .55 our put option would have a delta of -.45
Together they equate to stock:
Buy call: the right to buy the stock + Selling put: The obligation to buy the stock.

Our call option with a delta of .55 tells us that our option gives us the equivalent of 55% of the underlying value or an equivalent share position of 55 shares. Our put options with a delta of -.45 would equate to 45% of the underlying share. Making a total of 100% the underlying.

Gamma: (δ) Measuring the movement of Delta

Option has a Delta of .63
Option has Gamma of .145
If underlying rises or falls by $1.00 then
Options Delta will rise or fall by .145
Upside new delta of .775
Downside new Delta of .485

Long (buy) options: positive gamma
Short (sell) options: Negative gamma

Long gamma means that as the stock goes higher/lower you get longer/shorter
Short gamma means that as the stock goes higher/lower you get shorter/longer

Theta: (θ) The passage of time

The loss in value an option will experience due to the passage of time. This number is expressed on a per day basis. If an option has a theta of .018 it means that with all else remaining constant (stock price, volatility and interest rates) the option will lose 1.8 cents per day of time value.

Vega: volatility measure

The change in an options price based upon the change in the options implied volatility expressed as a dollar value. If an option has a Vega of .15 and the implied volatility changes by 1%, the options value will change by 15 cents.

Rho: (ρ) Interest rates

Interest rate effect on option prices

Increasing interest rates will DECREASE put values and INCREASE call values on a risk neutral basis.

Decreasing interest rates have the opposite effect.
Rho is independent of volatility.

Alpha: γ/θ

Alpha is the ratio of Gamma over Theta. Alpha indicates the relative value of owning gamma relative to the current level of theta. It is a measure that allows for comparison of several different options on the basis of how much they cost daily to own (Theta) versus the potential gamma derived return (profits from movement) from owning them. The greater absolute value of Alpha the more potential for profits exists against the loss from Theta for long positions. The converse is true for short positions.

19

Back Spread Front Spread, Ratios for all

ABC
Stock price: 35.50
ABC June 35 Calls $2.50
Delta .61

Back spreading is a way to take advantage of market movement with limited risk. In the above example the ABC June 35 calls are worth $2.50
Intrinsic value $2.00
Time value: $.50

The Delta of the June 35 call is .61

When first learning about new option strategies we should be as neutral as possible. We therefore want to implement this strategy from a point of neutrality. We don't care if ABC Shares go up or down. We just want them to move from where they currently sit.

Our position would be as follows:

"ABC June 35 Calls, $2.50 Bid for 5"

We buy 5 ABC June 35 calls for a price of 2.50 ($1250.00US)

"Sell 300 ABC at 35.50 short"

We sell short 300 shares of ABC

	ABC	-300
+5	June 35 Calls	
	June 40 Calls	

This type of positioning allows us to take advantage of violent market movements.

At Expiration

ABC Stock price 50
June 35 call price 15.00
June 35 Call delta: 100

Stock profit/loss: -$4,350.00
Option profit/loss: =$6,250.00
Net P/L: +$1,900.00

ABC Stock Price 25
June 35 Call price: -0-
June 35 Call Delta: .00

Stock profit/loss: +$3,150.00
Option profit/loss: -$1,250.00
Net P/L: +$1,900.00

ABC Stock price 35.00
June 35 Call price:-0-
June 35 Call Delta: .00

Stock P/L: +150.00
Option P/L: -$1,250.00
Net P/L: -$1,100.00

Back spreading allows the option investor to control risk while allowing for unlimited profit potential.

If the concept of selling stock short is a problem or just new, you'll have to get used to it. You can initiate a position in a stock by selling it "short" without owning the stock.

Depending on the size of your margin account, you get paid short interest on your margin balance when you sell stock short. When you borrow money on margin you pay interest. When you have a credit balance you receive interest.

If the underlying security is not short sellable then we go back to the synthetic relationships.

Backspread position if short stock not available:

"ABC June 35 Calls $2.50 Bid for 5"

We buy 5 ABC June 35 calls for $2.50

ABC June 30 puts buy 3
ABC June 30 Calls Sell 3

We establish a synthetic short stock position using the June 30 calls and puts.

Front Spreading positions: In a word the opposite of back spreading. Buy/write strategies are front spread positions.

The options floor world was divided into two camps : front spreaders 65% and back spreaders 35%. I was a member of the back spreading camp. It was easier for me to know my risk at all times. However the back spread camp is only 35 %. Most market makers love selling premium. You know how much money you should collect every month. The problems arise when the markets have violent moves.

We were trading on the Amex floor in the XMI pit. Don, a colleague of mine, was a front spreader and had sold over $350,000.00 in premium for the month. The market was due to close in 15 minutes.

At 3:45 p.m. EST in NY, Don stood to make over $300,000.00. At 4:15 p.m. when all settled in the XMI index, he was down $1.3 million. Suffice it to say the XMI index moved a lot more than Don thought it would. He knew I was flying to the office in Chicago that afternoon so he asked me to tell the clearing firm what happened. It wasn't a pleasant experience for me so you could imagine what it was like for him. He was asked to leave the firm. He has, since then, done quite well but it's just one of the things that can happen.

For back spreaders it can be just as bad, just over a longer period of time. I went through what I refer to as my five-week boot camp. Because of premium decay I lost $5,000.00 a day, every day for five weeks. That included weekends. Premium decay doesn't rest when the weekends roll around. Those are extreme examples. Both camps also enjoy days where profits abound. It becomes a matter of using both strategies when the time is right.

Strategy Implementation:

1. Learn the synthetics
2. Use conversions, reversal and boxes to determine overvalued and undervalued options
3. Back or Front spreads – (a) Are you more comfortable with limited risk and unlimited profit potential? (b) are you more comfortable with limited profit potential with unlimited risk? Once you know that, find out if you're (c) comfortable with breaking even or possibly losing money nine months of the year for the potential of three months of absolutely dynamic profits or (d) making steady money for nine months of the year, knowing that there will be three months where you could lose all that you made in the prior nine months.
4. Stick to your risk and money management profiles
5. Follow the CBOE VIX index as a gauge of volatility in the market place

Learning about options teaches more than you think. You begin to see the finance industry in a different light. It makes you realize that there is a lot more potential out there than first thought.

Risk Management: How much pain can you take?

As an option trader you should know what your money risk is at all times. Many option traders are taught this by the array of software out there that will tell you all "the numbers".

The real way to look at it is quite simple and you don't need fancy software. A person with a $100,000 equity account should risk no more than 2-3% on any one trade.

That means if you purchase a stock for $10,000 and attach a trailing stop order of 20%, you're willing to lose $2,000 or 2% of your total account.

It doesn't mean that you can only invest 2% or $2,000 per trade.

20

Socially Responsible Investing (SRI)

There are people out there who want to invest their money in companies that are good for their psyche. SRI, as it's called, applies screens on individual stocks, bonds and mutual funds. The screens can be positive or negative in scope. They let an investor screen companies on the basis of:

Human rights: Hiring practices of the company in the area of race, religion, and sexual preference. Can also cover animal rights.

Defense and Weapon Technology: Screening companies that are in the business of selling and manufacturing military hardware, satellite systems, ground and or space based weapon technologies e.g. HAARP

Alcohol & Tobacco: Companies that manufacture these drugs of choice for quite a few people

Nuclear Power: Not just weapons but companies that use nuclear power as an energy source

Environment: Polluters on land, sea and air... Companies and their policies on the greenhouse issue and logging.

Labor Relations: A company's record on dealing with the unions that represent the workforce

Gambling: Casino stocks are a no-no...

Killer Companies: Companies that at some point in time manufactured products that caused the death of workers. There are 70 to 100 companies, some still publicly traded, that over the past 50 odd years literally killed part of the workforce with asbestos. Some of these companies provide fair compensation to these workers and their families. Most companies do not. The nasty companies try to hide behind government legislation and legal trickery to literally get away with murder. The company directors will say that they have a responsibility to their shareholders. Don't believe it.

When a company goes bankrupt:

a. Creditors (bond holders) are first on whatever is left in the food chain.
b. Preferred shareholders are next in line to feed.
c. Common shareholders are last.

They are just trying to pay out the least amount possible and will even look to compensate their lawyers handsomely for saving them money. You'd be surprised to see what companies would be on the list. In Australia, James Hardie is one of those companies.

It's heartening to watch the Australian workers unions protesting against the company. By doing that *en masse*, the media, deeming it news worthy, has decided to cover the story. 15,000 workers marched on the Australian Stock exchange in Melbourne, Victoria. Union members also used advocacy.

The members purchased shares in James Hardie N.V. and attended the shareholders' meeting in the Netherlands, the company's new corporate refuge. In the US, companies like Worthington, Johns Manville (now owned by Berkshire Hathaway), Pfizer subsidiary Quigley, 3M, Halliburton and Westinghouse, to name a few, are in similar positions. These companies had foreknowledge of what their products would do.

The US government under the guise of helping individuals get compensation, wanted to establish an asbestos fund to compensate victims and their families about six years ago. The monies to fund this would come from the companies involved with asbestos. In actuality, it was a slush fund to alleviate the companies from paying millions of dollars to their victims. The payout for a person with mesothelioma would be one million dollars over three years from the government asbestos fund. Ah well, so much for expediency. The average person diagnosed with mesothelioma has a life expectancy of two years. Currently through the courts, the payout is on the order of four million dollars. So companies through their lawyers and lobbyists were attempting to get the government to make a deal for them at a rate of 25 cents on the dollar. US Senators Orrin Hatch and Arlen Spector, who put this legislation forward, thought people didn't realize what was really going on. It had nothing to do with fair compensation. It's about protecting companies at the expense of individuals. As my father used to say, "The companies lobby and the Congress bends over."

As a market maker on an exchange floor, there is no time to be a shareholder advocate but for some of the investing public, it is important. Shareholder advocacy allows the investing public to really take an active role. Personally, I believe in screening out companies because of what they do or don't do. Being that I no longer trade on the floor, I would be an advocate, buy the minimum amount of stock allowed, attend the shareholders' meeting and legally voice my opinion before the board. If I invest in a company that would be considered an SRI no-no, I'd then take some of the profits from the trade and donate them to a cause… I think that's the better way.

Let the company's profits fund the activist movement. What it comes down to from an energetic standpoint is right action. We are responsible for our deeds. Companies should be commended for the good works they do and responsible for the harm they do just like individuals should be. This may happen in principle but in fact... Some companies literally get away with murder.

21

Government

Is the government on your side?
Simply put – no.

"We the People" means individuals fall through the cracks. It is impossible for a government to concern itself with the needs of an individual. We are currently living in a time of major conflict. Folks are worried about security of hearth and home. I for one tend to look at our current situation as a test.

Why at this point in time have we not risen to the point where the populous is clothed and fed? How is it that people are still homeless? Why has the education system reached a level of apathy and disdain not heard of before? In other words, why are people not satisfied with their life?

Let's run an experiment. Every adult member of the population is to be given the following: 10 acres of land; any house you want; any car you want; and $100,000 to spend how you want.

Barriers will be put up around the acreage and no one is allowed to see anyone else's stuff until everything is ready. We all work meticulously on the house plans and finally every house is built. We pick our rides and are ready to go out shopping with the $100,000.

Ready, Set, GO.... The barriers are lifted and everyone takes off in their cars. They see what their neighbors have built and drive and say, "Why didn't I think of that?" How can we expect government to fulfill our needs when we aren't sure what we want?

President George W. Bush in one of his 2004 re-election speeches said "Government isn't about making people rich..." That is a fact. The government doesn't want you to be rich. The government needs you right where you are doing what you're doing. It needs you working and hungry. Talk to any politician and they'll say that their constituents want them to make sure that the roads are maintained etc. That means that government's main concern is that infrastructure is there for its citizens.

If you're lucky enough to really see what is going on out there early in the piece, you start to reject all of the dross as just that... an impediment to what you really want.

As you trade and see fundamental numbers fail then technical analysis like Fibonacci levels, volatility bands and moving averages let you down, you start to look for what really works. You notice that the markets are people and their ideas.

Back in the '80s one of the specialists on the floor said something that was an introduction to what I like to call right thinking. We were in the cold war, and nuclear winter was in the public consciousness. Folks were talking about a run on the banks and a market meltdown.

One of the specialists said that if that were to happen he would buy every stock he could. I asked him why.

He said, "Well, if there is a nuclear war, New York is over and we're all dead anyway. If there were no conflict then I'd have purchased stocks at bargain basement prices and would make an absolute fortune when everything started back up."

Needless to say we averted the conflict.

Then another question arose. Why would a person who trades short term for a living buy and hold stocks for a long time? That's easy to answer now.

Good companies consistently make money and that's how you can build generational wealth. Re-invest the dividends and let them run.

The world has been coming to an end for many decades now. Yet, in spite of all the gloom and doom, we're still evolving. The ups and downs along the way just help us get there. Experiences are the key. A person or a society that just wants equanimity is slowing down their evolution.

22

Support Mechanisms

Support – who supports you and how do you honor them.

Synchronicity…

What does spiritual life have to do with trading? To some people not much. If you even mention a supreme being to some people they'll say that they don't believe and they don't want to hear that stuff, especially if you're talking about finance. For me it is quite simple. I do not want to work with people who believe that this creation happened by chance. Why? It's time for a story.

My grandfather was an alto sax player by the name of Hilton Jefferson. He played in the bands of Fletcher Henderson, Cab Calloway, Duke Ellington and others in the '20s, '30s, '40s and '50s. He passed away in 1968. My brother and I were very young and our parents decided that we would not attend his funeral. My older sisters went.

We are Catholic and I figured that the service would be at the Catholic Church. It wasn't. It was held at the Masonic Temple on Amsterdam Avenue and 153rd St. in Manhattan.

I would later find that fascinating because I've not heard of many funerals being held at the Masonic hall.

When I later decided to play bass guitar along with saxophone, my mother gave me a phone number to call. It was a person that my grandfather worked with. His name was Milt Hinton. Over the years I got to know Milt and gained a lot of respect for him and his bass-playing prowess. I was given the use of a pre-CBS fender precision and a Rickenbacher 4001 for practicing, along with a three-quarter scale German blonde bass that was well over 100 years old. My relationship with Milt was a tonic for me as I learned a lot about my grandfather from him. Now that I was older I could appreciate the stories.

1994 Ganeshpuri India

While at the ashram a person by the name of Illinois Jacquet showed up. He was a devotee of Gurumayi and well known in the ashram community. Being that he played in the same bands as my grandfather I decided to go up and introduce myself. I walked up to him and said, "Mr. Jacquet, I'm..."

"You're Jeff's grandson Matthew. Milt Hinton told me you were over here."

After I picked my jaw up from the floor we had great conversations over many days. Of all the ashrams in India, let alone the world, this kind of synchronicity exists. Milt and Illinois lived a couple of blocks from each other in Queens, NY. Illinois told Milt he was going to India and Milt told him that I was there in an ashram somewhere and to say hello when he saw me. Milt was also a Mason. Life is filled with many of these stories. For me they are signals that I'm on the right path.

Someone asked me why I didn't trade for others. That question led to a ten-year journey of discovery. At one level, trading for others is a waste of time because they would look at my risk tolerance and have a stroke. On another level my broker dealer license forbade trading for public customers. Another reason and a very important one is that the public is not honest with themselves about trading. They want the proverbial magic pill. They want to buy a stock for $100 dollars on Monday and have it worth $10,000 dollars on Friday.

Later in life I tried working with the trading public. The public has been programmed/brainwashed by the establishment to the point where fear rules. When what you can lose is more prevalent than what you can make you're doomed.

I've debated whether or not to say this here... Yes was the answer. As I sit here writing this, I'm now compelled to tell what I believe to be the real reason behind my journey.

While trading on the floor, the question I asked myself was: does this trade serve my purposes? In hindsight it should have been, does the floor still serve my purposes?

San Francisco California 1995

After returning from India and my spiritual practices, I was given a boon. This gift would explain everything that I'd done this lifetime prior to that trip and would tell me what my purpose was in the so-called future. This kind of experience is more than just life changing. It is life revealing.

I normally would go to sleep around 10:30 p.m and wake up at 5:00 a.m to get ready for the trading day. This week, however, would be different. I will not go into every experience that happened this week because it's not necessary but every morning at exactly 2:57 a.m. I went ... traveling.

I mean I was literally pulled out of my body and was taken to different places. While in these places I was taught lessons about myself and about this creation we call the universe. Now some would say these could have just been dreams.

I can say with certainty that they were not dreams. This happened every morning at the exact same time and I would physically wake up before leaving.

I was enveloped in a scintillating blue light and off I would go. I met beings of many orders that taught me lessons. My Guru also taught me in these realms. I really began to look forward to going on these journeys. I'd wake up, turn my head to look at the clock and say, "Ah, 2:57 a.m, here we go." I can tell you that this experience was life-changing. What I was taught was beyond profound. But... my last journey is the one I will mention.

I was once again taken on a journey but this one was different. The blue light and I took off, and I was placed in a log cabin. The cabin was a non-descript room with four walls and a roof – nothing very spectacular to look at. Inside the cabin, someone that I knew was working as a caretaker for this cabin. It was my brother Martin. He was mopping the floor as I walked in. There was a silver bucket half full of water. In the center of the bucket floating on the water's surface was what looked like a small piece of blue soap.

I acknowledged him and proceeded out a back door to a garden. I turned to my right and saw a being seated on a high-backed wooden chair. I knew who this being was. Not by name, I found that out a few years later. I knew what order in the spiritual hierarchy this being was from. I approached this being and out of respect, bowed before him. The being reached out and blessed me.

I am not at liberty to fully describe what happened after this blessing. What I can say that while in this state there was no time. There was no past and there was no future but more importantly there was no present either. To describe that state in any of those terms is incorrect. I can say that this experience gave new meaning to the words "I am." The earth we now call home and the galaxy that contains it was a speck smaller than an angstrom unit somewhere off in the distance. And that distance was beyond vast. Yet at the same time it was as close as a thought.

I did not come back to body consciousness in the same way as the other times. As I came back to my body I was aware of it fully. It was done in a way to let me know in no uncertain terms that I was not my body. I was so much more.

It allowed me to fully understand what had just happened. I immediately got up and wrote down this experience.

After that everything changed. It was as if every spiritual practice I did up to that point lead to that blessing. And even with that I knew it was the grace of the Gurus that truly allowed that being to bless me in that way. I also knew that a blessing like that comes with a responsibility.

The first thing that came to mind for me was a question. This question took me three years to answer. Was the whole reason for my going to the floor of the stock exchange a spiritual initiation? The answer was yes. That meant that I no longer had to be there. The purpose for my going through all those experiences on the floor had been served. I knew that my path was elsewhere. This didn't mean that I would retire to a cave to meditate. It meant that I could now honor that life choice, knowing it led me where I needed to be. It also showed me that the holy beings have compassion. Allowing my initiation to take place on the floor, so to speak, gave me the tools to support my family and myself as I pursue my spiritual practices.

That experience comes from doing spiritual practices, probably over many lifetimes, and from being of service to others. I know that if that is my true state of being, it also the true state of all. We all come from that same source. That means I have a duty to perform. That duty is to make as many people as possible aware of that fact. The reason we learn to meditate, contemplate and chant is to serve.

After this experience I had a new outlook and goals to match it. As soon as I ask questions that truly serve me, the universe sends me the answers. Meditation and Spiritual practice can be mystical or technical depending on the school and teacher chosen. I wanted to be able to go back to that state of consciousness: what I know as my true state of being. That desire led to a path that could explain it and allow me to continue the journey.

Grand Master Choa Kok Sui, founder of modern day Pranic healing and Arhatic yoga, says, "Truth is beyond correct information. It is being able to see the different facets and levels of a certain event or object, and to act accordingly, properly, and kindly..."

Finding a teacher that can bring that understanding into focus is a must. Then you have to do the work. For me that work continues.

Trading options is easy, not difficult. Peel away the layers of dross that have been placed there by individuals who have an agenda and see the levels of truth therein.

I have retired from public trading. I trade only for myself and for family. My service to the financial community is to teach how I was taught to look at the financial markets. This writing endeavor is to let people know that there is a purpose to all this financial stuff. What that purpose is depends upon where you are on your path right now.

For me the path is the acceleration of my spiritual evolvement. The tool is trading options stocks and bonds. The profits allow me to serve others in a way I enjoy while funding my travels which bring me to spiritual evolution. My reasons are my own. The tools and strategies can be used by anyone. The foundation must be anchored firmly so that the structure will withstand the upheavals that inevitably come to pass.

23

The Path Chosen

The Trading on the floor of a stock exchange can be one of the most stressful endeavors to undertake.

It may seem that these two things, trading and meditation are polar opposites. They are not. When you meditate, when you truly understand why we are here on this plane of existence you start to understand what is actually happening. We are spiritual beings. We are the "divine spark". We are God's image in this physical plane. What does that mean God's image? It's quite simple actually. If everything is God then God is everything.

God exists everywhere. Some individuals, however, want to separate from that existence and thus control what happens here.

If you have clear vision, if you meditate asking for clarity, you will truly see. So how do you do this? Throughout the ages there have been stories of holy men enduring arduous tasks to reach the state of perfection while in human form. Ancient texts are full of stories of how a Yogi stood in a frozen lake in the mountains using the hatha yoga asana called tree pose for decades to reach a state of liberation. The story then continues by saying the Gods in the heaven worlds started to worry that the yogi's actions would lead that yogi to a position of authority over them so they sent a temptation to, shall we say, use up the merit gained by the yogi's actions.

That temptation usually came wrapped in the form of a beautiful woman. The story usually stops there but what does it truly mean? How is it relevant to our current way of life? The connotation of that story is that the yogi will see this beautiful woman and abandon his quest for perfection because the woman now represents that perfection in human form. He will then let his lower nature take over and have, using today's vernacular, a dirty weekend, month, year and /or decade. In the process said yogi will abandon his spiritual pursuits and the Gods in the heaven worlds can once again relax knowing their positions are secure until the next Yogi heads for the lake.

What is the Yogi giving up? Is the Yogi giving up anything? If he accepts the Gods' offering, taking on the responsibility that comes with it, then yes he is giving up something.

Spiritual Term – Life force.

Physical Term – Semen

Use – On a physical level, the act of meditation starts a process in which seminal fluid in males travels up the spinal column from the lower energy centers to the brain where it is spiritually transmuted and used as food for the higher energy centers. Male semen fertilizes female eggs to create human life on the mundane level. Its spiritual essence however is life itself. It helps to create and solidify the connection between the Soul and the Higher Self.

It's the reason why sexual activity should be regulated. It's also the reason why sexual activity is promoted and encouraged by multi-national companies and businesses world-wide. Wasting life-force hastens the body's demise. That means less time to reach our spirit's true purpose which is the reason we incarnated here to begin with. The so-called human gods [elitists] here have less to worry about and their positions remain secure

The stock exchanges and that life style in the '80s and '90s could be as decadent as you wanted it to be. You literally had enough money [energy] to indulge in whatever activities you wanted to. But in the midst of all that was spirit. As if the universe was offering you whatever path you wanted. The universe created it all for us to learn from so it makes sense that in the midst of hedonism's central hub, another path was offered. A path leads to the higher self. A path leads to the divine source of all things. And that path has just as many diversions as all the others.

Meditation practice for me is a way of life. So much is made of meditation these days for one reason. That reason is control. When you start to look for a meditation practice you need to remember what the goal is. Meditation doesn't give you anything. You already have everything you need. Meditation takes away that which you don't need in your life.

That can be quite disconcerting at first so that's where the words humility, awareness and compassion come in. There are so many meditation techniques. There are also many religions that are trying to explain the same concept to different people who have different cultures and speak different languages.

Meditation is attuning your body so you can witness all the dualities of this world and go beyond them to the absolute. Once you understand that, you appreciate all the little games being played by the masses and their overlords. And there was no better place to watch that game than from a stock exchange floor.

Meditating takes time to learn properly. Meditation also is about experimentation. You experiment with the direction you face. You experiment with how you sit. You experiment with what time of day is more powerful. So many things to consider but the key word is experimentation.

So you first do your own research then you ask people you know about it. They tell you about a guy that knows a girl that has a teacher who learned from so and so many years ago and they are teaching classes. You could fill the supermarket aisles with all the different meditation techniques out there. So what really works?

You could fill volumes with the work people have done over the decades. For a person that wanted to fulfil and honor his family's spiritual heritage and excel in the markets the following worked for me.

Daily Practice

Wake Up Time: 5:30a.m.
Meditation: Wool Blanket half lotus posture
Direction: NNE compass point 25 degrees
Technique: Internally bow to the four directions N-S-E-W then above and below

Deep breathing: expanding the lower rib cage and lungs [yogic breath] for 3 minutes then breathe normally. Invocation: Thank my inner guides and spiritual teachers.

Chakra activation – Basic, Heart, Crown and Brain

Hand Mudra: [Kubera] – Thumbs, Index and middle fingers touching with ring and pinky folded in on palm of hands. Hands comfortably placed on lap.

Mantra: Mantra repetition to center the mind.

Many believe that meditation is done to quiet the mind. Well, the opposite happens at first. Every thought known to man comes up. That can lead to frustration beyond measure. Then you get pains in your extremities. Then you hear all these sounds. Sounds that you used to consider background noise and would ignore at any other time are amplified. If a butterfly were flying by outside you'd hear its wings flapping.

Consider this the universe's way of testing your resolve. Don't even try to stop the mind from thinking. Let the thoughts come then, and this is important, let them go. Just be aware of the breath and the mantra.

I would do this for one hour in the morning and one hour at night. At night I would activate different chakras, use different mudras and face a different direction. Over the years I've adjusted and learned from spiritual teachers that I trust how to subtly improve these techniques.

As you continue meditating you start to see changes happen. They are not dramatic changes at first. It's more like: I used to have a drink after work but I haven't done that for a couple of weeks. You then try to go back and pinpoint the moment when that shift occurred.

I can tell you that you won't find it and you don't need to. As I stated earlier meditation takes away what you don't need in your life. As you continue, more and more will drop away. Meditation does a spring cleaning so to speak on your consciousness leaving only what truly matters to your soul's development.

It does such good work that it gives you clear focus to the point where you recognized that New York City and all it contains must be spring cleaned. That is quite difficult for one person to do on their own so you pack up and leave.

Meditation removes apathy and passiveness from your energy field. You see the truth and all that comes with it. You no longer have to mull over decisions about life choices. You act because those actions allow your spiritual advancement. You see manipulation for what it is and the financial markets are manipulated in more ways than you care to imagine.

You are put in places where your spiritual evolution can proceed. And you don't live life based upon other people's perceptions. In New York, I had a front row seat to watch governments and financial institutions manipulate the options, futures, bond and forex markets for their own benefit.

I was able to see and understand the control mechanisms that were put in place. I saw how the control of information flows meant power and equity for a select few. That could seem harsh to the average person but when you see it through spiritual eyes there is a dramatic difference. You see the game for what it truly is, just a game.

A game is something people play to entertain themselves. It's a way of engaging others using a set of rules to see who can come out on top. When adults watch children playing a game, they do so with different eyes. They remember being a child and playing. They remember how some children would cheat. They remember how some children would react violently at the outcome because while playing that game it was real.

But as an adult you recognize it as just a game. There are lessons about engaging with other children, learning how to play fair etc. The outcome might make the victorious child feel good for a couple of minutes but then they are bored and need something else to do. The adult who is spiritually aware recognizes that life on this plane of existence is another game. There are spiritual children who cheat and react violently at life's outcomes because while playing this game they believe it to be real.

They learned this behavior from their parents who were spiritual children and knew no better. As my teacher used to say "immature fruit comes from immature trees". There does come a time however where we as individuals make a decision to change. We decide to follow a different path. We see the game for what it is. We try to tell others what we have learned. Some of the others listen. Most of them are not quite ready to hear that kind of information and ridicule it out of hand.

So what makes us follow that different path this time? What allows us to finally see what is going on? What wakes us up to the fact that it is a game being played? It's quite simple actually. After lifetimes of taking on human form and living out the definition of insanity, we simply change the premise. And that little change gives us a different result. And that different result is enough to shift our perception dramatically.

The simple act of taking a few deep breaths and de-focusing your eyes before reacting to a situation allows you to actually see what is happening around you. It helps you maintain clarity. It also suspends the time component. When you actually experience that everything is happening now and time is just a concept the world changes.

It is a dramatically different path. It would seem that stock exchanges are the last place you would find any of this. What would options trading have to do with any of this? Well, options trading is the three sided pyramid. On the top of the pyramid you have the absolute form. On the bottom left and right you have the dualities that together represent that absolute. The core of options trading is just another variation of an ancient spiritual theme. The underlying security [top of the pyramid] has its dualities known as calls [the right to own] and puts [the right to sell]. They are based on the absolute but are individual entities as well. [See chapter 13]. They must always equate to each other and the absolute.

When you add in the concept of time you realize just how false time is. Anyone who trades options knows this. We spent day after day trying to price time. Time is outside of the pyramid and depending on who you talk to, time was valued differently. But… in the end time has a value of zero. In the end the bottom sides of the pyramid once again expire and merge into the absolute until the next cycle when they are created again.

This pattern is found in many walks of life. Based on that, the pattern or path is open to many people. I guess the universe is waiting patiently for people to realize this. As you reach out to learn the universe reaches out and moves you along the path. It's truly fascinating watching children play but after a while you get up put the game away and get on with life.

For the people that want to keep playing please knock yourselves out. For the people who want to keep evolving: stop relying on mainstream industries to truthfully provide for your wellbeing. If you are waiting for a time they will announce the next phase of human evolution and the way forward, forget it. The powers that be know the true value of time in the mundane world.

Epilogue: A Path

Leaving NY in '98 was a brilliant move; only I cannot take the credit for it. Spiritual intervention was key. I physically would get ill if I stepped on the Amex floor. My spirit would no longer allow me to dwell in that 'snake pit'. My heart rate literally would peak at 200 beats per minute to the point where my physician asked on more than one occasion if I were taking illicit drugs. I wasn't. What would calm me down was meditating. It became a major part of my daily life. And as I meditated more and more, many things became crystal clear. Not just about the thieves on Wall Street but about corruption on every level in government.

One thing that must be mentioned here: Members of the stock exchanges had a loathing for all members of the financial community that were considered to be "off the floor". If you worked as a retail stockbroker, banker, analyst or back office person with any of the big banks or firms, you were one of *them*.

When the FALN* was setting off bombs in the late '70s early '80s on the weekends in front of the Merrill Lynch building near Trinity Place and threatening to do it during trading hours, the offices were evacuated but not the trading floor. The regulators attitude was "keep those markets going". I found out five years after the fact that on two occasions we were left on the trading floor during bomb scares while the offices were emptied. What kind of wonderful human beings would allow that? Just take a look at who runs the big firms, banks, and government regulatory agencies and you'll have your answer.

As for what happened to all those characters that made up the trading floor – well, some did quite well for themselves but for others, it ended badly. You see, a lot of the big name Wall Street firms were covertly bigoted to the core in the '80s. I know that sounds like a cop-out but it was a fact and in some cases still is standard operating procedure today. Bear Sterns, Merrill Lynch, Shearson Loeb Rhodes, SLK, AG Becker and Dillion Reade were all suspect when it came to racist hiring practices. Also, a few small specialist firms left a lot to be desired as well.

As for the regulators in Washington DC, dear God! The "word" was that if you couldn't make it in the private sector, you worked for the government. If a firm wouldn't hire you as an attorney in M&A, you could work for the SEC and get payback through regulation. That could then lead to an even better job five to seven years later in private industry depending on whether you looked the other way while those companies flouted the law. Those big firms could not get away with all they do without government help so to speak. Yet in spite of all that, universal consciousness and spiritual awakening happened on Wall Street for many people. And that awakening told me it was time to leave.

I left all that for San Francisco and the Pacific Stock Exchange. I decided I would take the train so I could see the United States up close. What I found was the trip showed me the US in a different way. I took this trip with my spirit eyes wide open. From New York City we travelled north toward the cities of Albany and Buffalo. I would describe the journey using the color scheme of brownish grey. A very subdued and stifling feeling hung in the air as we continued north. Into Pennsylvania then Ohio we travelled. The energy of old steel towns whose time had come and gone was quite thick. The colors outside matched the colors inside the train carriage: dark browns, burnt orange and steel grey.

Indiana greeted me with blue skies. This meant I could really see the browns and greys. Bright green weeds were rising up through old grey bricks which made up factories that were no longer in use.

The Amtrak train continued westward to Illinois. Quite an uneventful run into Chicago. I used to live on Marine Drive in the city but today that didn't matter. Today Union Station Chicago was a transit area. I disembarked and headed for the platform to catch the California Zephyr.

As I boarded the train for the continuation of my journey, my spiritual eyes and my brain still were evaluating the journey just taken. The analysis: The Northeast corridor of America was used up, neglected, dreary, dark and dank. I was happy to be moving on. But also a feeling of gratitude arose. I lived there for the first 28 years of my life. I had a great time in spite of my recent analysis. Spiritual growth was taking place because I looked upon the positives and negatives with equal fondness.

The Zephyr left Union station heading west. How would this part of the journey unfold? Spiritual eyes at the ready. Well, at first not much changed. We travelled along through farm country towards the Iowa border. The crossing of the Mississippi River meant leaving two-thirds of the US population behind me. I was now more alert and aware of my surroundings.

I looked down upon the waters of the Mississippi River. The surface was glistening dark blue. I felt a tangible shift in the energy as the train crossed over this beautiful life sustaining river.

The internal information I was getting on a spiritual level had shifted. It wasn't because I had never been there before. I had been to California many times as well as Iowa. This was an energy shift. This was farm country. Growth... Life. I started to see a difference. The air was even different. The heaviness was starting to lift. The greens became bright and vibrant. Then the subtle yellow brown and greens of the cornfields dominated. Beautiful farmhouses came into view.

The train pulled into Ottumwa which immediately brought up memories of the television show M*A*S*H and the character Radar. Things that make you smile.

I was more physically and spiritually aware of the energy difference. The Zephyr continued westward. Next we arrived in the State of Nebraska. And back to the color beige-brown. But it was a different brown. There were wheat fields and expansive vistas. The train stopped in Lincoln. I wanted to get out and stretch my legs for a bit. I had never been in Nebraska before so I wanted to physically stand in the space. Even as I write this I still see a beige – brown and sandstone palate.

On to the State of Colorado and the Rocky Mountains. Here, everything opened up.

The difference was physically dramatic. The skies were the bluest blue. The air was crisp. As we travelled further westward, it started snowing. Also the air took on that February chill. Because of the snow and cold, the tracks contracted and the train could travel no faster than 30 mph.

The universal energy was saying relax, take it slow and enjoy. I got a real good look at my surroundings. As I write this, my mind's eye can see the skiers coming down a run in Winter Park. It's still that vivid. Winding through the Rockies towards the State of Utah, I saw my first Bald Eagle take off from a tree as the train rounded a bend towards a tunnel outside of Glenwood Springs.

Most of the trip to Utah would be at night time because of the speed restrictions but the Rocky Mountains put on quite a show. Next stop, Salt Lake City. We arrived late morning welcomed by beautiful blue skies. The train, from memory, would break up into three lines here.

One would head towards Las Vegas, one would head towards San Francisco and one would go northwest towards Seattle. As the train left Salt Lake City and headed into the desert, I had a hard time describing the colors. I then thought of the full moon on a clear night. That color of grey was as close as I could get to describing the landscape. Beautiful blue skies with a moonlike grey soil.

We travelled across the Bonneville Salt Flats westward towards Winnamucca Nevada. The ground started taking on a more red clay-like appearance the further west we travelled. It now reminds me of the Uluru area of central Australia. The spiritual feeling of this area however was quite draining unlike Ayers Rock/Uluru. Quite frankly I was looking forward to stopping in Reno to relax. The train pulled into Reno at night and we got a bit of a rest.

Before long, we were heading westward again. It was the home stretch. Ahead of us was California. Through Truckee, Sacramento and finally into the Bay Area in Oakland/Emeryville. San Francisco is one of the most beautiful cities on earth let alone the US. From an energy standpoint there is spiritual abundance in the Bay Area and its surrounds. A lot of that energy comes from the people who live there. I got to experience the energy patterns of the US on that trip across the country. In general terms there is more life force in certain areas than in others. This trip showed me that once again I was in tune with what I needed for my spiritual evolution. I'd call the family and some friends once I settled in.

Some of the traders on the floor thought I was mad for even contemplating such a move. "Why would you go to that Mickey Mouse exchange?" My reasoning was simple, at least to me. I love computers. I spent $3,800 on my first IBM 256K monochrome screen computer with two 5¼ inch floppy drives and a dot matrix printer back in 1984. But hey, it came with all the bells and whistles and a beautiful brown boxed version of DOS. Then the XT and AT systems came along.

The programming I was able to do was fantastic at the time and the computer paid for itself in one month quite easily with winning trades based on my volatility sheets generated using that computer. So to me, Silicon Valley and the Bay Area made sense. And my timing was spot on! I arrived in San Francisco on one of the few snowy days in the city's history. The street I lived on was populated by transplanted New Yorkers. Life was as beautiful as my Haight Ashbury neighborhood. But what about back in NY? Wouldn't the market makers back there want to get in on the ground floor of the tech boom? One word: blinders. When you are on Wall Street in New York City, Philadelphia doesn't exist, let alone San Francisco. 'Total' financial awareness, at that time, stopped at the Mississippi River.

New York was the center of the known universe and nothing else mattered. California is full of hippies, surfers and freaks. From a financial standpoint back then, California didn't matter.

Well, now the American Stock Exchange is no more. It was amalgamated into NYSE Euronext and buried. A lot of former members who didn't like Black people, but loved money even if it came from the Black Caribbean drug dealers needing laundry services, breathed a sigh of relief when that exchange closed down.

You see, some of the former members died under dubious circumstances because of their greed. Others committed suicide. Nine of them went down with the World Trade Centre on 9/11. Most of them just left the industry because the floor is for 20- and 30-year-olds, not 60- and 70-year-olds. Some still trade off-floor now. But all in all, what little good karma the place had was used up.

There was another group that was extremely happy about the Amex closing. All the big brokerage firms were happy. They'd be even happier if the NYSE closed as well. Why? Quite simple, actually.

There was one thing that just about every market maker knew when it came to the trading floor. The big firms hated the place. You see, firms like Goldman Sachs and Merrill Lynch have enough clients on both sides of the market. They could do all the trades in-house through their trading desk. But the fact was that stock exchange floors were the arbitrary third party, a witness to two sides creating a contract. That's the last thing the big brokers and the banks want. It gets in their way. It's an annoyance that should be eliminated.

The Banks and big brokers have spent the last three decades doing everything in their power to declaw the stock exchanges. They already have the regulatory agencies and government under tow. Today's markets with computer algorithms running rampant are all the big boys need to control the Western World's Financial Purse

The Pacific Stock Exchange at the time represented, to a certain extent, freedom from all that east coast treachery.

San Francisco was fantastic. It had great trading floor, good people, and better hours because of the time difference. Nine great years of floor trading would follow. Then it happened. Technology stocks took a rocket ride. The Pacific Stock Exchanges volumes tripled. Options contracts on the tech group of stocks became the number one traded contracts even, in some cases, surpassing volumes on the CBOE and the AMEX.

It was inevitable that the following would happen. A few of the guys who told me I was nuts for leaving New York appeared on the Pacific Exchanges option floor looking to set up shop. I said to Pat, who was an options market maker with me back in NY, "What the hell are you doing here?"

"Hey Matt! Yeah this place is really booming. We're looking to set up an operation out here."

That's all I needed to hear. I spent the next six months winding down my positions because it was time to leave. By 1998 off floor technology was starting to pick up and trading rooms were beginning to open up for market makers who had enough of the pits. My time as a professional Market Maker was about to end.

I left as the New Yorkers hit the floor. Seat prices went from 25K when I started in '89 to 300K when I left in '98 so that was a nice trade.

The markets continued on for a bit. Seat prices spiked up to $485,000 dollars on the high. But you can guess what happened next. As I said, they used up all their good karma back in NY. The New Yorkers got their operation up and running in '98-'99. Welcome to the Dot.com bubble. Timing is indeed everything!

Sixteen years of floor trading. What remains from that experience? This is the world of duality. The spiritual path shows you both sides fully. Then you get to choose. But quite frankly there was no choice, at least for me. I chose the spiritual path long before I arrived in San Francisco. That path was patient enough to work with me so I could say goodbye and properly end that chapter of this life.

Trading is a part of me that is a constant to this day both in theory and in practice. Meditation and contemplation are even bigger parts of my life now. My father Emmett has passed on and graduated from this spiritual school with honors, as have most of the gentlemen from the Doral Bar. One of my spiritual teachers, Grand Master Choa Kok Sui, has also made the transition to higher dimensions. All of them imparted lessons that fortified me and more importantly showed me where I am going.

The American Stock Exchange and the Doral Bar are both no more. The Amex showed me good and evil. The Doral Bar helped me interpret the dualities on that floor and find correct expression. Both places are still alive in me as are the lessons they imparted. They along with the PSE were the launching pad for what is to come… Blessings be upon them.

M.R. Adams

*FALN: The FALN (Armed Forces of National Liberation) is a clandestine organization committed to the political independence of Puerto Rico from the United States. Between 1974 and 1983, the FALN claimed responsibility for more than 120 bombings of military and government buildings, financial institutions, and corporate headquarters in Chicago, New York, and Washington DC.

Website: http://www.encyclopedia.chicagohistory.org/

Bibliography

Fernández, Ronald. *Prisoners of Colonialism: The Struggle for Justice in Puerto Rico.* 1994.

Torres, Andrés, and José E. Velázquez. *The Puerto Rican Movement: Voices from the Diaspora.* 1998.

Zavala, Iris M., and Rafael Rodriguez. *The Intellectual Roots of Independence: An Anthology of Puerto Rican Political Essays.* 1980

Glossary of Option Position and Order Types

Order Types

AON (All or None) An order that must be filled in its entirety or not at all.

Contingency Order An order which becomes effective only upon the fulfillment of a predetermined condition or conditions in the marketplace.

FOK (Fill or Kill) An order which will be automatically be cancelled unless it can be executed immediately and in its entirety.

GTC (Good 'til Cancelled) An order to be held by a broker until it can be executed or is cancelled by the customer.

IOC (Immediate or Cancel) An order that will automatically be cancelled if it is not filled immediately. An IOC order need not be filled in its entirety.

MIT (Market if Touched) A contingency order that becomes a market order if the contract trades at or beyond a specified price.

MOC (Market on Close) An order to be executed at the current market price as near as possible to the close of that day's trading.

Market Order An order to be executed immediately at the current market price.

Not Held An order submitted to a broker, but over which the broker has discretion as to when and how the order is executed.

OCO (One Cancels the Other) Two simultaneous orders, either of which may be executed. If one order is executed, the other is automatically cancelled.

Stop Order A contingency order that becomes a market order if the contract trades at a specified price.

Stop Limit Order A contingency order that becomes a limit order if the contract trades at a specified price.

Trailing Stop Order A contingency order that tracks the closing price of a contract on a daily basis and adjusts its price accordingly.

> E.g. Buy 1000 XYZ @ 25.00 with a 10% trailing stop on Monday.
>
> If the XYZ drops 10% ($2.50) a market order is entered to sell XYZ.
>
> If XYZ closes at $26.00 the trailing stop price is adjusted to 10% of the closing price ($2.60) on Tuesday.
>
> If XYZ then closes at $29.00 on Wednesday, The trailing stop will be based on 10% of $29.00 (2.90)

Option Positions

Back Spread A spread, usually delta neutral, where more options are purchased than sold, and where all options have the same underlying contract and expire at the same time.

Bear Spread Any spread which will theoretically increase in value with a decline in the price of the underlying contract.

Box A long call and a short put at one exercise price, together with a short call and a long put at a different exercise price. All options must have the same underlying contract and expire at the same time.

Bull Spread Any spread that will theoretically increase in value with a rise in the underlying contract.

Butterfly The sale (purchase) of two options with the same exercise price, together with the purchase (sale) of one option with a lower exercise price and one option with a higher exercise price. All options must be of the same type, have the same underlying contract, and expire at the same time, and there must be equal increments between exercise prices.

Buy/Write The purchase of an underlying contract together with the sale of a call option on that contract.

Calendar Spread See Time spread.

Christmas Tree A spread using three exercise prices. One or more calls (puts):

are purchased at the lowest (highest) exercise price and one or more calls (puts)

are sold at each of the higher (lower) exercise prices. All options must expire at the same time, be of the same type, and have the same underlying contract.

Combination Most commonly used to describe a long call and a short put, or a short call and a long put, which together make up a synthetic position in the underlying contract.

Condor The sale (purchase) of two options with different exercise prices, together with the purchase (sale) of one option with a lower exercise price and one option with a higher exercise price. All options must be of the same type, have the same underlying contract, and expire at the same time, and there must be equal increments between the exercise prices.

Conversion A long underlying position together with a short call and a long put, where both options have the same exercise price and expire at the same time.

Covered Write The sale of a call (put) option against an existing long (short) position in the underlying contract.

Diagonal Spread A long call (put) at one exercise price and expiration date, together with a short call (put) at a different exercise price and expiration date. All options must have the same underlying contract. A time spread using different exercise prices.

Front Spread A ratio vertical spread.

Horizontal Spread A time spread.

Iron Butterfly A long (short) straddle, together with a short (long) strangle. All options must expire at the same time and have the same underlying contract.

Jelly Roll A long call and short put with one expiration date, together with a short call and a long put with a different expiration date. All four options must have the same exercise price and the same underlying contract.

Ratio Spread Any spread where the number of long market contracts (long underlying, long call, or short put) and short market contracts (short underlying, short call, or long put) are unequal.

Ratio Vertical Spread A spread, usually delta neutral, where more options are sold than purchased, and where all options have the same underlying contract and expire at the same time.

Ratio Write A covered write using more than one option.

Reversal A short underlying position together with a long call and a short put, where both options have the same exercise price and expire at the same time.

Time Spread A long call (put) at one exercise price and expiration date, together with a short call (put) at the same exercise price but different expiration date. All options must have the same underlying contract.